Mere Christianity:
Discussion and Study Guide
For the Book by C. S. Lewis

By

Joseph McRae Mellichamp

Scripture references are taken from the NEW AMERICAN STANDARD BIBLE®, Copyright © 1960, 1962, 1968, 1971, 1973, 1975, 1977, 1995, by the Lockman Foundation. Used by permission.

To the guys of Daybreak for Men in Atlanta, Georgia,
For whom these notes were developed.

Mere Christianity:
Discussion and Study Guide
For the Book by C. S. Lewis

Book 4. Beyond Personality: Or First Steps in the Doctrine of the Trinity

MERE CHRISTIANITY
Introduction

In April of 2000, *Mere Christianity* was named the most important Christian book of the last century by *Christianity Today*. Unfortunately, many people are reluctant to attempt to read this magnificent classic. Why is this? I think many are intimidated by C. S. Lewis' reputation as a scholar—they think they might not be up to his intellectual arguments. And this is simply not true. It is a challenging read to be sure, but most people can, with a bit of effort, understand the book and be encouraged by it.

I spent twenty-five years of my life as a professor in the university and most of my effort in teaching was focused on attempting to make difficult subjects simple so that students could master them. Several years ago I determined to apply that talent to *Mere Christianity* so that businessmen in a group I teach here in Atlanta, Georgia, might enjoy and understand and be encouraged by this wonderful book. These discussion and study notes are the result of that effort. I hope you enjoy reading the book, with my notes, and perhaps discussing the material and my questions with friends in a small group. So let's get started. First, a few comments and then Book 1, Chapter 1.

If one wished to write a defense of the Christian faith, there are several approaches he or she could take, all of which would be effective. Here are some possibilities:

- One could present scientific evidence for the existence of God.
- One might share his or her personal experience with Christ.
- One might show Old Testament prophecy and its fulfillment in the New Testament.
- One might describe all the good the Christian faith has accomplished.

C. S. Lewis passes over all of these approaches and builds his case on human behavior. The effectiveness of his approach over those suggested above is huge—here are just a few of the benefits:

- The presentation begins as a discussion of philosophy, not religion.
- The notion of God is not addressed until well into the discussion.
- Lewis relies on logical arguments rather than citing religious writings.
- He eliminates all worldviews except Christianity, including:
  - Atheism,   - Agnosticism.
  - Pantheism.   - Materialism.
  - Dualism.   - Darwinism.
  - Judaism.   - Islam.

Lewis has arranged Books 1 and 2 so that there is a natural filter at the end of each book, which requires the reader's buy-in before proceeding to subsequent ideas. It is important that we know what these filters are and see them as "hinges" for the logical arguments Lewis is making.

Here is the filter for Book 1: "Christianity only speaks to a person who realizes that there is a Moral Law, there is a Power behind the Law, he has broken the Law and put himself wrong with that Power." [See page 17 in these notes]

Here is the filter for Book 2: "Christ was killed for us, that His death has washed out our sins, and that by dying He disabled death itself." This is what Lewis claims is Christianity; this is what has to be believed in order for one to be a Christian. *This is mere Christianity*. [See page 35 in these notes.]

In the material that follows I have included for each chapter a detailed chapter outline, a brief chapter summary, and several discussion questions. Enjoy the journey!

Book 1. Right And Wrong As A Clue To The Meaning Of The Universe

1. The Law of Human Nature

Quarreling

We can learn something very important from the things people say when they are quarreling:
- "How'd you like it if someone did the same to you?"
- "That's my seat, I was there first."
- "Leave him alone, he isn't doing you any harm."
- "Why should you shove in first?"
- "Come on, you promised."

All such talk is appealing to a *standard of behavior* that one expects the other person to know about.

And the standard responses to such statements usually fall in one of two categories:
- The offender argues that his behavior really doesn't go against the standard.
- The offender offers excuses as to why his behavior is exempt from the standard.

The Rule of Fair Play

When people are involved in disputes:
- They act like a law or rule of morality is in force.
- They both are agreed on what is right and wrong.
- They try to demonstrate that the other is in the wrong.
- Without some agreement, there is no sense arguing.

The Law or Rule about Right and Wrong has various names:
- The Law or Rule of fair play.
- The Law of Decent Behavior (Morality).
- The Law of Nature.
- The Law of Human Nature.

All individuals are governed by certain laws, with one important distinction.
- Individuals are absolutely bound by physical laws, e.g., gravity.
- Individuals can choose to obey or disobey the Law of Nature.

The Law of Nature was called this because:
- People thought that everyone knew it and did not need to be taught it.
- People thought that it was obvious to everyone.
- Different civilizations in different ages have similar ideas of right and wrong.

Whenever individuals or nations say they don't subscribe to the Law, they betray their core beliefs by appealing to "fairness" in matters of conduct.

Thus, Lewis concludes that we are forced to believe in a real Right and Wrong.
- Some people may sometimes be mistaken about the specifics.
- The Law of Human Nature is not a matter of taste and opinion.

Our Performance

None of us is really keeping the Law of Nature. And two very curious attributes of the law are:
- The moment anyone tells me I am not keeping it, I start making excuses for myself.
- We believe in decency so much we cannot bear to think that we are breaking the law.

Summary of Chapter 1

- There is a law of Human Nature or Right and Wrong. (Moral Law)
- None of us are keeping the law of Human Nature.

Questions

1. Do you really believe that most people live as though they believe that there is a Rule of Decent Behavior in operation that constrains themselves and others to act in mutually respectful ways?

2. In postmodern times, we often hear the mantra, "Well, that may be right for you, but it isn't necessarily right for me." This is really just an excuse for bad behavior, but there are a surprising number of people in our culture who think this way. Does this kind of thinking obviate Lewis' argument?

3. How would you respond to someone who has bought into this particular way of thinking? Is there any way you can think of that would expose their inconsistent logic? Any examples you might use to cause them to see the error in their thinking?

4. Lewis challenges us to think of a culture in which morality is totally different from our own. Our morality might be characterized as Western civilization. What about terrorists who believe they have a mandate to kill their opponents?

5. In an Appendix to *The Abolition of Man*, Lewis includes a study of the moral codes of many of the ancient civilizations of history including Chinese, Near East, Norse, Egyptian, Jewish, Roman, Greek, Babylonian, Anglo-Saxon, and American Indian and also Christian and Hindu moral codes. He suggests from this eight moral principles that are thus common to all people of all times. What is your reaction?

6. When asked by a legal expert to identify the greatest commandment in the law, Jesus replied, "'You shall love the Lord your God with all your heart, and with all your soul and with all your mind.' This is the great and foremost commandment. And a second is like it, 'You shall love your neighbor as yourself.'" He went on to suggest that these two propositions contain all moral law. What do you say?

7. Lewis makes two important points in this chapter—(1) that humans all over the earth think they ought to behave in a certain way, and (2) that none of them believe they behave that way. He then makes a remarkable statement. "These two facts

3

are the foundation of all clear thinking about ourselves and the universe we live in." Do you believe this? Why or why not?

2. Some Objections

The Herd Instinct

Some people believe that the Moral Law is simply our herd instinct and is developed like all of our other instincts. There are several arguments why this can't be true:

- There is a difference between being prompted by instinct and being prompted by the Moral Law.
  - Being prompted by instinct means having a strong urge to act in a certain way.
  - Being prompted by the Moral Law involves feeling that one *ought* to act in a certain way.

  The thing which judges between two instincts cannot be either one of them.
- When we are most conscious of the Moral Law it usually seems to be telling us to side with the weaker impulse. We cannot be acting from instinct when we make an instinct stronger than it is.
- There is none of our impulses which the Moral Law may not sometimes tell us to suppress. There is no such thing as good and bad impulses.

The most dangerous thing you can do is to take any one impulse of your own nature and set it up as the thing you *ought* to follow at all costs.

Social Convention

Other people argue that the Moral Law is just a social convention, something that is put into us by education. Here is why this cannot be true:

- Some of the things we learn are indeed social custom, like driving on the right side of the road. But some are *real* truths, like physical laws and mathematical principles.
- Here are some reasons why the Moral Law is *real* truth:

- The moral ideas of one time or one country are very similar to those of other times or countries.
- We can judge between the morality of one people or country and another. If no set of moral ideas were truer or better than any other, we would be indifferent between differing ideas of morality.
- The standard that measures two things is something different from either. Whenever we begin to compare two different moral ideas, we admit that there is a Real Morality, independent of what people think.
- If the Rule of Decent Behavior meant simply "whatever each nation happens to approve," there would be no sense in saying that any one nation had been more correct in its approval than any other.

Summary of Chapter 2

- The law of Human Nature or Right is not just our herd instinct.
- The law of Human Nature or Right is not just social convention.

Questions

1. What are some of the natural instincts that you follow every day? Is any one of these better in any sense than any other?
2. Do you ever experience times in which you are aware of yourself overruling one impulse in favor of another? Would you share your experience with the group? Is the impulse which was overruled a bad impulse?
3. Have you ever found yourself wishing that you had followed some impulse that was in conflict with another? Would you share that experience with the group. Why do you suppose you feel as though you might have done the wrong thing by not following your conscience?
4. Give an example of where picking one impulse and setting it up as that which ought to be followed at all costs would lead to

a bad end. Can you imagine any scenario where doing this would be a good thing absolutely?

5. The word "ought" is a simple one—we use it often, usually without thinking. What does the word mean? What does it imply?

6. How would you compare the morality of modern day America with that of Victorian England? What are you admitting the moment you begin to make your comparison?

7. How would you compare the morality of modern day America with that of the Taliban? Of al Qaida?

8. How would you compare the morality of modern day America with that of the Kingdom of God as described by Jesus in the Sermon on the Mount in Matthew 5-7?

3. The Reality of the Law

The Law Applied

Two points from Chapter 1 are worth reviewing at this point:
- People are haunted by the idea of a sort of behavior that they *ought* to practice, we call this law fair play or decency or morality.
- No one is really keeping the Law of Human Nature.

Now, what exactly does it mean to break the Law?
- You might say that breaking the law only means that people are not perfect and this is true, but not very helpful.
- What are the consequences of something being imperfect, of its not being what it *ought* to be?

The answer to this depends on the "something" we are thinking about:
- If we are speaking of stones or trees, they are what they are, and it is senseless to say that they ought to have been otherwise. The laws of nature applied to stones or trees only means what nature does. We call these results facts.
- The Law of Human Nature applied to humans does not mean "what humans beings do," but what they *ought* to do and do not do. And when we are dealing with humans, something else is in play beyond the actual facts.

So in the case of humans, we have the facts (how men do behave) and we have something else (how they *ought* to behave).

Explanations

This phenomenon is so peculiar that we are tempted to explain it. Lewis gives the following illustration to help; a man who gets a choice seat on the train because he got there first and a man who got the seat because he slipped in while Lewis had turned away for a moment. Lewis says, and we would all agree, that he blames the second man and does not blame the first. This leads Lewis to ponder the nature of behavior; what makes behavior good or bad?

- Sometimes the behavior we call bad is not inconvenient to us—it does not necessarily harm us. So we cannot say the behavior we call decent is only that which is useful to us.
- And as for decent behavior in ourselves, it should be obvious that we're not talking about behavior that pays. Some examples:
  - Being content with making 50k on a deal when we might have gotten 75k.
  - Being honest on our taxes when it would be easy to cut corners.
  - Staying in a dangerous place when we'd rather go to a safer place.
- Some say that though decent conduct does not mean what pays each particular person at a particular moment, it means what pays the human race as a whole.
  - Humans know that you cannot have any real safety or happiness except in a society where everyone plays fair.
  - Because most people understand this, they try to behave decently.

But this notion really misses the point—according to Lewis, it is circular reasoning. So he concludes by saying that men *ought* to be unselfish, ought to be fair, period. The Law of Human Nature then can be said to have these characteristics:

- It is not simply a fact about human behavior.
- It is not a mere fancy—we can't get rid of the idea.
- It is not how we would like others to behave for our own convenience.
- It is a real thing, not something we invented.

Summary of Chapter 3

- There is a different kind of reality apart from the facts of men's behavior.

- There is a real law of decent behavior which is pressing in on all of us.

Questions

1. Can you give an example of anyone who is not bothered by the fact that they are not keeping the Law of Human Nature? Can you give an example of anyone, apart from Jesus of Nazareth, who is keeping the Law or who kept it perfectly?
2. Do you understand the difference between the facts of how we behave and the something else, the how we ought to behave. Do you see that these are clearly different things altogether?
3. Give an example of bad behavior on the part of someone else that is not harmful or inconvenient to you. Do you understand why we would label this as bad behavior? What should be your response in the face of this bad behavior?
4. Give an example of good behavior on your part that affects you adversely. Do you see why we wouldn't call this bad behavior just because it affected you negatively?
5. Lewis' complaint with the argument explaining that people act decently because it is in the best interests of society as a whole is a subtle one indeed. Can you explain why this is a circular statement?
6. Lewis makes the very important point that the Law of Human Nature is a real thing. What does he mean by this? Do you believe this—that this law is a real construct, that it isn't just something we imagine?

4. What Lies Behind the Law

How Did the Universe Come to Be?

Here is what we have established about the Law of Human Nature thus far:
- It is something above and beyond the actual facts of human behavior.
- It is a real law which we did not invent and which we know we *ought* to obey.

Ever since the beginning of the human race, men have puzzled over what the universe really is and how it came to be there. Two views have been held:
- The Materialistic View.
  - Matter and space just happen to exist, and have always existed. No one is sure why.
  - Matter behaves in certain fixed ways, why this happened is just a fluke, but very fortuitous for humans.
  - Our solar system is another fortuitous happenstance. One of the planets just happened to have exactly the right conditions for life.
  - Somehow, again no one knows exactly how, some of the matter on planet earth came alive.
  - By a long series of chances (evolution), the living creatures developed into things like us.
- The religious view.
  - What is behind the universe is more like a mind than it is like anything else we know.
  - It made the universe, partly for purposes we don't know, but partly to produce creatures like itself—with the ability to reason.

Don't think that one of these views (religious) was held a long time ago, and the other (materialistic) has gradually taken its place. Both are held by thinking men.

11

Why is There a Universe at All?

One cannot discover which of the two views concerning what the universe is and how it came to be by science in the ordinary sense.
- Science fundamentally works by experiments—by observing how things behave and then by making inferences based upon the observations.
- Science cannot answer questions concerning why anything exists at all and whether there is anything behind the things science observes.
- If there is "Something Behind," then it will have to remain altogether unknown to men or else make itself known in a different way.

The statement that "there is any such thing," and the statement that "there is no such thing," are neither of them statements that science can make.

Lewis asserts here that there is one thing, and only one thing, in the whole universe which we know more about than we could learn from observation. That one thing is Man. And here is what we know about man:
- Men find themselves under a moral law.
- Men did not fabricate the law and they can't forget it.
- Men know they *ought* to obey this law.

So the real question before us is whether the universe simply happens to be the way it is for no reason or whether there is a power behind it that makes it what it is. That power, if it exists, would not be one of the observed facts but a reality which makes them; no mere observation of the facts can reveal it.
- Thus, if there was a controlling power outside the universe, it could not show itself to us as one of the facts inside the universe.
- The only way in which we could expect it to show itself would be inside ourselves as an influence to get us to behave in a certain way.

Lewis uses the illustration of a postman delivering letters to prove the point. He writes, the only letter I am allowed to open is Man. When I do, especially that particular man called Myself, I discover (1) that I do not exist on my own, (2) that I am under a law, and (3) somebody or something wants me to behave in a certain way.

Summary of Chapter 4

Lewis warns the reader that he is not within a hundred miles of the God of Christian theology. Here is what we have so far.

- Something like a mind is directing the universe—it couldn't be matter because matter doesn't give directions.
- This Something appears in us as a law urging us to do right and making us feel responsible and uncomfortable when we do wrong.
- The fact that we have something in us urging us to "do the right thing" is evidence that the second view of how the universe came to be is correct.

Questions

1. Most scientists and intellectuals in the U.S. today believe in the materialistic view of the universe; yet almost 90 percent of the general population accepts the religious view. Where do you stand?
2. Do you think we could dress up the language Lewis used to describe the materialistic view to make it a bit more palatable? Why or why not?
3. Do you understand why science can't answer questions about the purpose of the universe or how it came to be? Do you think the average man or woman in the street understands this?
4. Do you agree that we know more about man than about any other part of the creation? Do you know more about yourself than any scientist could ever know by observing you? Do you agree with Lewis' assessment of your situation?
5. Do you agree with his statement that if there is a controlling power outside the universe it couldn't show itself to us as one

of the facts inside the universe? See Romans 1:19-20. Explain the apparent contradiction.

6. Do you understand the claim that the fact that we have something in us urging us to "do the right thing" is evidence that the second view of how the universe came to be is correct? Can you explain this?

5. We Have Cause to Be Uneasy

From the previous chapter, Lewis concludes that the existence of the Moral Law would lead us to conclude that somebody or something from beyond the material universe was actually getting at us. And he suggests that our reaction to this might be twofold:

- Some might feel a certain annoyance. They might rather be left to themselves to do what they jolly well want.
- Others might feel that Lewis had pulled a bait and switch—he started talking about philosophy and then switched to religion.

Philosophy or Religion?

Has the discussion really shifted from philosophy to religion? Lewis has three things to say to anyone who thinks so.

- Some say, "The world has tried religion and it didn't work, you cannot turn the clock back." Lewis argues that when you look at the present [1943] state of the world, it is pretty plain that humanity has made a big mistake. Turning the clock back is a sensible thing to do when one discovers he has made a wrong turn.
  - We all want progress; especially in the sense of morality, or fairness, or decent behavior.
  - Progress means getting nearer to the place where we want to be—a return to civility.
  - If you are on the wrong road, progress means turning around and walking back to the right road.
  - The man who turns back soonest is the most progressive man. There is nothing progressive about being pig-headed and refusing to admit a mistake.
- Lewis argues that he is still talking philosophy—not religion. Several attributes of the discussion would confirm this:
  - We have not yet got as far as the God of any actual religion, certainly not the God of Christianity.
  - The only conclusion we have reached at this point is that there is a Somebody or Something behind the Moral Law.

- We have not taken anything from the Bible or the Churches, we are just trying to see how much we can find out about this Somebody on our own.
- So far, we have two bits of evidence about the Somebody.
    - The universe He has made. If this were our only clue, we should have to conclude:
        - That He is a great artist—for the universe is a very beautiful place.
        - That He is quite merciless and no friend of man— for the universe is a very dangerous and terrifying place.
    - The Moral Law which He put in our mind. This is more instructive than the universe. And we conclude from this evidence:
        - He is intensely interested in right conduct—in fair play, unselfishness, courage, good faith, honesty, and truthfulness.
        - That He is not 'good' in the sense of being indulgent, or soft, or sympathetic. There is nothing soft about the Moral Law, it is as hard as nails.
        - We have not got as far as a personal God—only as far as a power behind the Moral Law, and more like a mind than anything else.
- From the evidence, we can begin to make some inferences about the Somebody or Something:
    - If it is pure impersonal mind, there is no use in asking It to make allowances for us or to let us off.
    - If it is an impersonal absolute goodness, it would be foolish to conclude that you do not like Him and therefore were not going to bother with Him.
    - And here is the dilemma in which we find ourselves:
        - On the one hand we are on His side and really agree with His disapproval of human greed and trickery and exploitation. We know at bottom that unless the power behind the world really and unalterably detests that sort of behavior, then He cannot really

be good. If the universe is not ruled by an absolute goodness, then all of our efforts are hopeless.

   □   On the other hand, we know that if there does exist an absolute goodness, it must hate most of what we do. And if so, we are making ourselves enemies to that goodness every day so our case is hopeless again. He is our only possible ally, and we have made ourselves His enemies.

-   Goodness is either the great safety or the great danger— according to the way you react to it. And we have reacted the wrong way.

• In order to move beyond philosophy to something that will really help with the problem we face, several admissions must be made.

-   Christianity does not make sense until one has faced the sort of facts Lewis has been addressing.

-   Christianity tells us to repent and promises us forgiveness. It has nothing to say to people who do not know they have done anything to repent of and who do not feel they need forgiveness.

-   Christianity only speaks to a person who realizes that there is a Moral Law, there is a Power behind the Law, he has broken the Law and put himself wrong with that Power. [This is the first filter in the book. See question 7.]

-   Christianity offers explanations to our dilemma.

   ▪   It explains how we got into our present state of both hating goodness and loving it.

   ▪   It explains how God can be this impersonal mind behind the Moral Law and also be a Person.

   ▪   It explains how God Himself becomes a man to meet the demands of this law, which we cannot meet.

-   Christianity, in the long run, is a thing of unspeakable comfort, but it does not begin in comfort. It begins in the dismay Lewis has been describing.

Summary of Chapter 5

- We are on the wrong road. We need to turn back.
- We have only got as far as a Somebody or Something behind the Moral Law. If the universe is not ruled by an absolute goodness, our efforts are hopeless.
- Christianity only speaks to a person who realizes that there is a Moral Law, there is a Power behind the Law, he has broken the Law and put himself wrong with that Power.

Questions

1. Turning the clock back, if it were possible, might not be a bad thing to do, especially in the case of morality. What are some ways in which the morality or civility in this country has changed in the last 50 years; twenty-five years? What would you think of going back?
2. One of the definitions of the word progressive is "gradually advancing in extent"—applying this to morality, a moral progressive would be one who would be in favor of a more moral society. The question is how does one determine whether a society is advancing or decreasing in the extent of morality?
3. Do you agree that up to this point in the discussion, Lewis has not based any of his arguments or logic on Scriptures or anything taken from church doctrine? That is, that he has relied on simple statements of reason to get where we are.
4. Do you agree that the Moral Law is hard as nails? In what sense? Think of what Jesus said over and over in the Sermon on the Mount (Matthew 5-7), "You have heard that it was said ..., but I say to you ..." In every case Jesus was suggesting that the Law is more demanding than it appears on the surface. Given that this is the case, do you believe that any of us is OK according to the Law?
5. Why does Lewis write "unless the power behind the world really and unalterably detests that kind of behavior [human greed and trickery and exploitation], then He cannot really be good"?

6. What does Lewis mean when he says that "if the universe is not ruled by an absolute goodness, then all our efforts are hopeless"? Do you believe this?
7. In my mind, Lewis puts a very important gate in Chapter 5. Unless a person agrees with the following statement, "Christianity only speaks to a person who realizes that there is a Moral Law, there is a Power behind the Law, he has broken the Law and put himself wrong with that Power," there is no point reading further in the book. Do you agree? Have you personally come to this conclusion?

Book 2. What Christians Believe

1. The Rival Conceptions of God

To get the discussion started, Lewis suggests a couple of things Christians do not have to believe:

- Christians do not have to believe that all religions are wrong all through.
- Christians are free to believe that all other religions contain some hint of truth.

If one is an atheist, on the other hand, he must believe that the main point of every one of the world religions is wrong. And if one is a Christian, he must believe that where Christianity differs from other religions, Christianity is right and they are wrong. Some of the wrong answers, he notes, are much nearer being right than others.

Beliefs about God

All people can be classified according to their beliefs about God. The first division is between those who do not believe in God (atheists) and those who do (theists). [There is actually a third category—those who don't know or who haven't made up their minds (agnostics)]. Considering only those who do believe in God, there are two very different beliefs about what God is really like.

- Pantheists (Pantheism).
    - God animates the universe; He is what gives it life and substance.
    - The universe almost is God, so that if it didn't exist He would not exist.
    - Anything you find in the universe is a part of God.
    - God is beyond good and evil; everything is good in one way and bad in another.
- Monotheism.
    - God invented and made the universe.

- God is definitely "good" or "righteous."
- God takes sides; He loves love and hates hatred.
- God wants us to behave in a certain way and not in another.

If we don't take the distinction between good and bad very seriously, then it is easy to say that anything you find in the world is a part of God. If you think some things are really bad and God is really good, you can't talk like that. You must believe that God is separate from the world and that some of the things we see in the world are contrary to God's will.

The Christian view is that God made the world—that God conceived and created all things. But it also holds that a great many things have gone wrong with the world God made and that He insists, very loudly, on our putting them back right again.

What's Gone Wrong?

If a good God made the world, why has it gone wrong? One argument, the argument Lewis believed for many years, is that the world was not made by an intelligent, all-powerful God. His logic was that the universe seems so cruel and unjust. But the notion of justice became a fly in the ointment; from where does the idea of justice come? There are only two possibilities.

- It is simply a privately held idea—it doesn't really exist. But this logic creates a very troubling dilemma:
  - Conclusion: God doesn't exist.
  - Proof: The universe is cruel and unjust.
  - If justice is not a real construct, then the lack thereof (injustice) cannot be a proof against the existence of God.
- Justice is a real construct—it exists and men are aware of it. This view provides satisfying answers to the question of meaning.
  - Our whole notion of justice declares that the universe has meaning.
  - If the universe has no meaning, we should not be able to discern it

21

Summary of Chapter 1

Divisions in the Concept of God:
- Atheists.
- Theists:
  - God is beyond good and evil—Pantheists. God animates the universe.
  - God invented and made the universe. Christians believe things have gone wrong in the world and God insists that we set it straight.

If the universe has no meaning, we would never have discovered this—our whole notion of justice declares that it has meaning.

Questions

1. If Lewis is right that Christians don't have to believe that all religions are wrong all through, we should be able to make some true statements about non-Christian religions. What can you say that is true about Judaism? Islam? New Age religions?
2. One of the biggest points of contention between Christianity and all other religions is that the Scriptures teach that Jesus Christ is the only way to God (John 14:6, and other verses). How do you come down on this? What do we say to a sincere person like one of my neighbors, a Muslim, who said, "All religions are acceptable, they are just different ways to God?"
3. The Greeks were probably the most well-known Pantheists (many gods) in history—they had a god for every facet of life. In Acts 17:16-34, the Apostle Paul confronts the faulty logic of the Greeks in his famous address in the Areopagus. What can we learn from this discourse?
4. Many misinformed Christians have a problem with the Big Bang Theory. But this theory, which is widely held by most scientists throughout the world, argues forcefully that the universe had a beginning at a finite point in time. Since it had a beginning, and something cannot arise from nothing, it must

have had a beginner. What do you think now? Are you satisfied that God conceived and created the universe—from nothing?

5. Do you understand how playing "loosie-goosey" with the concepts of good and bad can lead to a wrong concept of God? Can you explain this to your group?

6. Lewis argues that justice is a real thing—it really exists and is not just an ideal in our minds. Can you explain how justice is actually a powerful argument for the existence of God?

7. Lewis infers from the notion of justice that the universe has meaning—our lives have meaning. How does he get from justice to meaning?

2. The Invasion

Simple Philosophies

Lewis wants no part of what he calls simple philosophies. He identifies a couple of them and tells us why they don't wash.

- Atheism is too simple—if there is no God and the universe has no meaning, we should never have found that out.
- Christianity-and-water is too simple. This is the notion that there is a good God in heaven and everything is OK. Forget all the difficult and terrible doctrines about sin and hell and the devil, and the redemption.

It is no good asking for a simple religion. And when we ask for something more than simplicity, it is silly to complain that the something more is not simple. Religion, Lewis says, is not something God invented, but His statement to us of certain unalterable facts about His own nature. Facts are reality, and reality according to Lewis is not simple, it is complicated, it is odd, it is not what you would expect, it is usually not something you could have guessed.

In fact, the complexity of Christianity is one of the reasons Lewis embraced it; it was not something men could have concocted. "It has just the queer twist about it that real things have," he writes.

By way of warning, Lewis notes that many critics of Christianity construct a straw-man version of Christianity (Christianity-and-water) and attack that. Then when one tries to correct them, they complain that if there really was a God, they are sure He would have made "religion" simple, because simplicity is so beautiful…

The Problem and the Answers

Here is the problem: there exists a universe which contains much that is obviously bad and apparently meaningless, and there are

creatures like ourselves who know that it is bad and meaningless. There are only two views that face all the facts.
- Christianity.
    - This is a good world [universe] that has gone wrong.
    - It still retains the memory of what it ought to have been.
- Dualism.
    - There are two equal and independent powers, one good and the other bad, at the back of everything.
    - The universe is the battlefield in which these two opposing powers carry on an endless war.

The Problem with Dualism

Lewis thought that next to Christianity, Dualism was the manliest and most sensible philosophy in the marketplace. But it has a fatal flaw in it.
- According to the philosophy, the two powers, or spirits, or gods—the good one and the bad one—have the following attributes.
    - They are supposed to be independent—of each other, and everything else.
    - They both have existed from all eternity.
    - Neither of them made the other.
    - Neither of them has any more right than the other to call itself God.
    - Each presumably thinks it is good and thinks the other bad.
    - One of them likes hatred and cruelty, the other likes love and mercy.
- The problem comes in when we call one of them the Good Power and the other the Bad Power. What does this mean? Either of two things:
    - We are merely saying that we prefer the one to the other—a matter of taste.
    - One of them is wrong, actually mistaken, regarding itself as good.
        - Regardless of what the two powers think.
        - Regardless what we humans happen to like.

25

Now if we mean we prefer one to the other simply as a matter of taste, then we must give up talking about good and evil altogether. If good simply means joining the side you happen to like at the moment, for no real reason, then good would not deserve to be called good.

So we must mean that one of the two powers is actually wrong and the other right. And the moment we believe this, we are admitting a third thing in addition to the two Powers: some law or standard of good to which one of the powers conforms and the other doesn't. Since the two powers are judged by this standard, then this standard, or the Being who made the standard, is farther back and higher up than either of them, and He is the real God.

And what we meant by calling them good and bad turns out that one of them is in a right relationship [conforms] to the real God and the other is not.

- Here is a different way to make the same point. If Dualism is true, then the bad Power must be a being who likes badness for its own sake. The nearest we can get to badness in life is cruelty; people are cruel for one of two reasons:
  - Because they are sadistic; they have a sexual perversion which makes cruelty a cause of sensual pleasure for them.
  - Because they expect to gain something from acting with cruelty—money, power, safety, etc.

The motivations for cruelty—pleasure, money, power, safety—are in themselves good things. The badness comes in pursuing them by the wrong method, or in the wrong way, or too much.

One can do good for the sake of goodness; one cannot be bad for the sake of badness. One can perform a kind deed when he is not feeling kind and when it gives no pleasure

26

because kindness is *right*. No one does cruel things simply because cruelty is *wrong*, but only because the cruelty is pleasant or useful to him.

Goodness, then, is itself; badness is spoiled goodness.

Thus, it follows that the Bad Power who is supposed to be on an equal footing with the Good Power and to love badness in the same way as the Good Power loves goodness is a delusion. In order to be bad he must:
-   Have good things to want and then to pursue them in a wrong way.
-   Have impulses that were originally good to be able to pervert them.

He must be getting both from the Good Power. If so, he is not independent. He is part of the Good Power's world: he was made either by the Good Power or by some power above them both.

- Here is an even simpler way to make the same point. To be bad, the Bad Power must possess:
-   Existence.
-   Intelligence.
-   Will.

But existence, intelligence and will are in themselves good. Therefore he must be getting them from the Good Power; even to be bad, he must borrow or steal from his opponent.

A Surprise

Now we can see why Christianity has always said that the devil is a fallen angel. This is not a fable; it is a recognition of the fact that evil is a parasite, not an original thing.

Lewis was surprised to find that the New Testament talks so much about a Dark Power in the universe—a mighty evil spirit behind death, disease and sin. Scripture teaches that this Dark Power was created by God, and was good when he was created, and went wrong. It teaches that Satan is not independent, and that there is a civil war in progress; we are living in a part of the universe occupied by the rebel.

Christianity is the story of how the rightful king has landed, you might say landed in disguise, and is calling us all to take part in a great campaign of sabotage.

Summary of Chapter 2

Views of Evil:
- Christian. This is a good world gone bad that retains a memory of what ought to be.
- Dualism. Two equal and independent powers are behind everything—one good and one bad power.

When you admit a Standard or Rule of Good, it is behind the powers of good and evil. Whoever made the standard is the real God.

Questions

1. Many philosophers believe that life has no meaning. An individual who does not believe in God also has to believe that life has no meaning. And if we follow Darwinism to its logical conclusion, we are also left with the notion that life is meaningless—we are just a genetic accident. Do you understand why atheism is too simple—or perhaps a better word is hopeless?

2. Christianity-and-water is a wonderful description of what some [perhaps most] people believe. There is a loving God in heaven, and everyone is going to live happily ever after in heaven with Him. Like a neighbor once who told us, "Of course I'm a Christian, I adopted two children, didn't I?" What would you say to someone who honestly believed in a Christianity-and-water religion?

3. The problem according to Lewis is: there exists a universe which contains much that is obviously bad and apparently

meaningless, and there are creatures like ourselves who know that it is bad and meaningless. Do you see how Christianity addresses the problem?

4. I don't know that I have ever engaged with anyone who seriously believed in Dualism—even in all my years in academia, the land of kooky ideas. Have you? Lewis, in my mind, has done a good job of putting Dualism to rest. Could you retrace his arguments in case you bumped into a Neanderthal who actually accepted this philosophy?

5. Lewis writes that he was surprised to read in the New Testament so much about a Dark Power. I'm sure he must have read Isaiah 14:12-15 and Ezekiel 28:12-17, which describe in detail Satan's creation and fall. Read these verses. Remember these passages. Do you see how crucially important they are in understanding what is happening in the world today?

6. I love how Lewis describes Christianity as "the story of how the rightful king has landed, you might say landed in disguise, and is calling us all to take part in a great campaign of sabotage." Are you aware that you are living in occupied territory? Are you engaged in a campaign of sabotage? How so?

3. The Shocking Alternative

Free Will

Christians believe that an evil power has made himself, for the present, the Prince of the World. The question this raises is. "Is this state of affairs in accordance with God's will or not?"
- If it is, one might certainly be justified in thinking that this is a very strange God indeed.
- If it is not, one would wonder how can anything happen contrary to the will of a being with absolute power.

Here's how. God created things which have free will. That means creatures which can go either *wrong* or *right*. If a thing is free to be good, it is also free to be bad. And free will is what has made evil possible.

Why, then, did God give His creatures free will? Because free will, though it makes evil possible, is the only thing that makes possible any love or goodness or joy worth having. The happiness God designs for his higher creatures is the happiness of being freely, voluntarily united to Him and to each other. For this they must be free.

Of course, God knew what would happen if they used their freedom the wrong way; apparently He thought it worth the risk. We might be inclined to disagree, but as Lewis points out there are problems in disagreeing with God:
- He is the source of all your reasoning power, it is impossible for Him to be wrong and you to be right.
- When we dispute with Him, we are arguing with the very power that makes it possible for us to argue at all.

If God thinks this state of war in the universe a price worth paying for free will—that is, for making a live world in which creatures can do real good or harm and something of real importance can happen, instead of a toy world which only moves when He pulls the strings we may be sure it is worth paying.

We might then ask, "Why did God make creatures of such weak stuff?" The better stuff a creature is made of—the cleverer and stronger and freer it is—then the better it will be if it goes right, but also the worse it will be if it goes wrong.

The Rebellion

How did the Dark Power go wrong? The moment you have a self at all, there is the possibility of putting yourself first—wanting to be the center—wanting to be God, in fact. That was the sin of Satan and that was the sin he taught the human race. Here are the specifics:

- Satan put in the heads of our ancestors the idea that they could "be like gods"—could set up on their own as if they had created themselves.
- Satan convinced them that they could be their own masters— they could experience some happiness outside God, apart from God.

And out of that hopeless attempt has come nearly all of what we call human history—money, poverty, ambition, war, prostitution, classes, empires, slavery—the long terrible story of man trying to find something other than God which will make him happy.

But Satan's plan will never work—here's why. God designed man for a very specific purpose:

- God designed us to run on Himself. He Himself is the fuel our spirits were designed to burn, or the food our spirits were designed to feed on.
- God cannot give us happiness and peace apart from Himself, because it is not there. There is no such thing.

Some fatal flaw always brings the selfish and cruel people to the top and it all slides back into misery and ruin.

God's Remedy

God, of course, knew from the beginning of time what would happen, and He had a remedy for the problem waiting to implement.

- He gave us conscience, the sense of right and wrong, and all through history there have been people trying (some very hard) to obey it.
- He gave the human race stories, scattered through all ancient religions, about a god who dies and comes to life again, and by his death gives new life to men.
- He selected one particular people, the Jews, and spent several centuries hammering into their heads the sort of God He was— that there was only one of Him and that He cared about right conduct.

The Old Testament is an account of the hammering process.

Then comes the real shock. Among the Jews a man turns up who goes about talking as though He was God. And He claimed much more:

- He claimed to be able to forgive sins.
- He claimed to be eternal.
- He claimed that He is coming again to judge the world at the end of time.

These were astounding claims for the following reasons:

- For the Jews, "God" meant the Being outside the world, who had made it and was infinitely different from everything else. When Jesus of Nazareth claimed to be God, it was, quite simply, the most shocking thing that has ever been uttered by human lips.
- For anyone other than God to claim to be able to forgive sins, is so preposterous as to be comic. Jesus told people their sins were forgiven, and never waited to consult all the other people whom their sins had undoubtedly injured. He behaved as if He was the party chiefly offended in all offenses. In the mouth of

32

any other speaker than God, whose laws are broken and whose love is wounded in every sin, these words imply what Lewis calls silliness and conceit unrivalled by any other character in history.

When we read the Gospels, we see nothing of silliness or conceit. We see One who is humble and meek. If He were merely a man, humility and meekness could hardly be attributed to some of His teaching.

Lewis suggests that his line of reasoning here is to foreclose on the possibility of anyone saying the really foolish thing that they often say about Him: "I'm ready to accept Jesus as a great moral teacher, but I don't accept His claim to be God." That is the one thing we must not say. A man who was merely a man and said the sort of things Jesus said would not be a great moral teacher. He would either be a lunatic—on a level with the man who says he is a poached egg—or else he would be the Devil of Hell. You must take your choice. Either this man was, and is, the Son of God: or else a madman or something worse. You can shut Him up for a fool, you can spit at Him and kill Him as a demon; or you can fall at His feet and call Him Lord and God. But let us not come up with any patronizing nonsense about Him being a great human teacher. He has not left that open to us. He did not intend to.

Summary of Chapter 3

- An evil power with free will has made himself Prince of this world.
- The sin of Satan was putting himself first—he wanted to be God.
- And this is the sin of humanity.
- God designed man to find happiness and peace in Himself.
- God sent His Son Jesus who claims He can forgive sin. He can forgive offenses against God only if He is God.
- We cannot simply say that He was a good teacher.

Questions

1. Many people have trouble with the concept of free will. Explain what the creation would have been like absent the attribute of free will. Now do you get it? Do you see why Lewis says that in order for there to be a *live* world, creatures must have free will?

2. Lewis says the price of free will is the state of war between good and evil. Who pays the price? Name some of the specific outcomes of the state of war.

3. "The moment you have a self at all, there is the possibility of putting yourself first—wanting to be the center—wanting to be God, in fact. That was the sin of Satan…" This is how Lewis describes the fall of Satan. Isaiah the prophet describes what we have come to call "the five I wills of Satan" in Isaiah 14:13-14. Where did Isaiah get his information? Did he get it right?

4. What does Lewis mean when he says, "God cannot give us happiness and peace apart from Himself, because it is not there. There is no such thing?" Do we try to find happiness in other things? Not just non-Christians, but Christians as well? Do you? In what sense?

5. The fact that there are salvation narratives in the cultures of many peoples throughout the centuries is well known. Many cultures, for example, have a flood story or narrative. Evidence of such a story is on display in the British Museum and is called the Epic of Gilgamesh. Did you know about such stories? What do you think of them?

6. Do you understand that the claims Jesus made, if He were not God, are, as Lewis calls them, preposterous? If you met someone today who claimed to be God, what would you think? What would you think if the person backed up His claim by raising someone from the dead?

7. Do you understand why we can't write Jesus off as just a great teacher? What must we do when we come face to face with who He really is?

4. The Perfect Penitent

A Frightening Alternative

We are now faced with what Lewis calls a frightening alternative:
- Either Jesus is exactly who He said He is: God.
- Or else, a lunatic, or something worse.

Lewis accepts the view that God has landed on this enemy-occupied world in human form.

What was the purpose of it all? A reading of the New Testament reveals a surface answer to this query and a deeper answer.
- Certainly He came to teach—the Gospels give us a comprehensive record of His teaching.
- But Lewis is struck by the fact that the Gospels are constantly talking about His death and His coming to life again.

It is obvious—Lewis says—that Christians think the main point of the story, the main thing He came to earth to do was to suffer and to be killed.

Lewis shares what he thought Christians had to believe before he became a Christian and then he clarifies that by expressing his post-Christian understanding of Christian belief:
- Lewis first believed that God wanted to punish men for having deserted and joined the Great Rebel (Satan), but Christ volunteered to be punished instead, and so God let us off.
- Lewis came to understand the Gospel in a much deeper sense—that Christ was killed for us, that His death has washed out our sins, and that by dying He disabled death itself.

This second statement is what Lewis claims is Christianity; this is what has to be believed in order for one to be a Christian. *This is mere Christianity*. [This statement is also the second filter Lewis has in the book. And as in the case of the first filter, unless the reader is willing to buy in to this statement, the rest of the book is not going to make a whole lot of sense.]

He suggests that there are many theories that explain how Christ's death accomplished everything it did and he goes on to present what he believes is the most likely explanation. He spends the remainder of the chapter describing the theory and suggests that if his explanation isn't helpful to drop it, since it is just an explanation of the thing to be believed and not the thing itself.

The Surrender

Now Lewis owns that the view that we are let off because Jesus has volunteered to bear a punishment instead of us is a very silly theory, thus he elaborates so we can understand it.

- If God was prepared to let us off, why on earth did He not do so? And what possible point could there be in punishing an innocent person?
- There is no point in the police-court sense, but if we consider things in some other light, it does make sense:
  - If we see the issue in the sense of a debt, it is reasonable for a person who has assets to pay the debt of someone who has no assets.
  - Or if we think of someone having got in a bind, so to speak, the trouble of getting him out usually falls on a kind friend.
- This way of thinking about the problem leads us to reconsider the kind of trouble we have got ourselves in:
  - We have tried to set ourselves up on our own, to behave as if we belonged to ourselves.
  - Fallen man is not simply an imperfect creature who needs improvement, he is a rebel who must:
    - Lay down his arms.
    - Surrender.
    - Say he is sorry.
    - Realize he is on the wrong road.

And having done so, start life all over again from the ground floor.

This process is called repentance, which Lewis says is no fun at all. It involves:
- Unlearning all the self-conceit and self-will that we have been training ourselves into for thousands of years.
- Killing part of our self, undergoing a kind of death—dying to our self as Jesus puts it in the Gospels.

Only a bad person needs to repent; only a good person can repent perfectly. The worse you are the more you need it and the less you can do it. The only person who could do it perfectly would be a perfect person—and he would not need it.

Repentance, this willing submission to humiliation and a kind of death, is often misunderstood:
- It is not something God demands of us before He will take us back and which He could let us off if He chose.
- It is simply a description of what going back to God is like. We can't ask God to let us come back without it.

But the same badness which makes us need to submit makes us unable to do it. We can only do it if God helps us—but what does this mean?
- He gives us His reasoning power, so we can see ourselves as He sees us.
- He puts His love in us, so we can love one another.

But there is a rub. We now need God's help to do something which God, in His own nature never does at all—to surrender, to suffer, to submit, to die. Nothing in God's nature corresponds to this process at all.

But suppose God became a man—suppose our human nature which can suffer and die was combined with God's nature in one person—then that person could help us. He could surrender His will, and suffer and die, because He was a man; and He could do it perfectly because He was God. So here is the bottom line:

- We can go through this process only if God does it in us.
- God can do it only if He becomes a man.

This is the sense in which He pays our debt, and suffers for us what He need not suffer at all.

One final point remains. Some complain that the suffering and death of Jesus was easy for Him because He is God. To this Lewis can only reply:

- This is a very odd reason for not accepting what He has done. His advantage is the only reason He can help.
- To what will you look for help if you will not look at that which is stronger than yourself?

Summary of Chapter 4

- The central Christian belief is Christ's death put us right with God.
- Christ was killed for us, His death washed away our sins, He overcame death.
- It simply requires repentance for God to take us back.

Questions

1. Lewis writes, "We are now faced with a frightening alternative: either Jesus is exactly who He said He is—God—or else, a lunatic, or something worse." Why is this a frightening alternative?
2. What would you say to someone who declared that the main reason Jesus came to earth was to teach—specifically, to teach us how to get along with each other? Could Jesus have accomplished His mission without teaching? Explain.
3. The difference between what Lewis thought Christians had to believe before he himself became a believer and what he understood after coming to know Jesus is subtle, but important.

Could you (open book, open note test) explain it to Joe Unbeliever?

4. Do you understand why God can't just let people off? This is precisely why those who think that everyone is going to heaven when they die are sadly and fatally mistaken. What would we conclude about God if this were the case?

5. There are those who truly believe that man is simply an imperfect creature who needs to "buck up" and try harder to be better. Do you see why this won't work? Have you come to the point in your own life where you realized as Lewis puts it you needed to surrender to God?

6. Repentance is absolutely crucial in the Christian faith. In the sense of salvation, repentance means to agree with God that one is a sinner, and to accept God's provision (the life, death, and resurrection of Jesus) in order to be reconciled to God. In the sanctification sense, repentance means to agree with God about some specific sin(s) and to accept His forgiveness made possible through the work of Jesus. Do you understand this? Could you explain it to Joe?

5. The Practical Conclusion

Christian Belief

Lewis concludes that perfect surrender and humiliation were accomplished by Jesus.
- Perfect because He was God.
- Surrender and humiliation because He was man.

Christians believe that *if* we share the humility and suffering of Jesus *then* somehow:
- We also share His conquest of death,
- We find new life after we have died.
- We become perfect and perfectly happy.

In logic, this is a conditional statement. The *then* part of the proposition is conditioned on the *if* part. Lewis will come back to consider what is required in order to share in the humility and suffering of Jesus. He does make clear that it means something much more than merely trying to follow His teaching.

To underscore that the Christian concept of man entails transformation, Lewis asks, "What is the next step in the development of man?"
- According to evolution—the step beyond man.
- According to Christ—the man indwelt by Christ.

How, asks Lewis, is this new life appropriated? How does it come to us? Here he is going to consider the *if* part of the conditional statement he presented earlier. Lewis believes the new life is appropriated in three ways, through:
- Baptism.
- Belief.
- Communion.

It is interesting that reformed theology speaks of the "means of grace" as being (1) the Scripture, and (2) the sacraments, i.e., baptism and the Lord's Supper. This would certainly affirm Lewis' view that belief, baptism and communion are the ways in which the life of Christ is appropriated by the believer.

Lewis writes, "… a Christian can lose the Christ-life which has been put into him, and he has to make efforts to keep it." What he means is that through neglect we can lose fellowship with Christ, not that we can lose our relationship with God which Jesus made possible. He notes some things that are true about Christians:

- A Christian is not acting under his own strength, he is to be nourishing or protecting a life that he could never have acquired by his own efforts.
- A Christian is not someone who never goes wrong, but someone who is enabled to repent and pick himself up and begin again after each stumble.
- A Christian has the life of Christ within which enables him to repeat in some sense the kind of voluntary death that Jesus Himself died.

So the difference according to Lewis between the Christian and others is:

- The unbeliever hopes that by being good, he can please God, if there is one; or if not, at least he hopes to deserve the approval of good men.
- The Christian thinks that any good he does comes from the life of Christ within him. He doesn't think that God will love us because we are good, but that God will make us good because He loves us.

Lewis affirms that Christians mean something very specific when they talk about the life of Christ in them:

- They don't mean something mental or moral; as, for example, following a moral code of ethics.
- It isn't simply a way of saying that they are thinking about Christ or copying Him; as, for example asking "What would Jesus do?"

They mean that Christ is actually operating through them; Christians together are the physical organism through which Christ acts—that we are His fingers and muscles, the cells of His body.

Some Objections

Now Lewis addresses two objections to the ideas that he has just explained:

- Is it not frightfully unfair that this new life should be confined [restricted] to those who have heard of Christ and been able to believe in Him? He answers as follows:
    - God hasn't told us what His arrangements for the other people are.
    - If you are truly worried about those people outside, the most unreasonable thing to do is to remain outside yourself.
    - If you want to help those outside, come inside to become part of His body; He alone can help those outside.
- Why is God landing in this enemy-occupied world in disguise and starting a sort of secret society to undermine the devil? Why is He not landing in force, invading it? Is it that He is not strong enough? Here is his answer:
    - We believe that He is going to land in force, we just don't know when.
    - He wants to give us a chance to join His side freely.
    - When God does interfere openly and directly in His world, it will be the end of the world. Then it will be too late to join His side.
    - When this happens it will be God without disguise; something so overwhelming that it will strike either irresistible love or irresistible horror into every creature.
    - Now, today, this moment, is our chance to choose the right side. God is holding back to give us that chance. It will not last forever. We must take it or leave it.

Summary of Chapter 5

- Christianity is more than just trying to follow the teachings of Jesus.
- Christ actually indwells believers and lives His life in them.
- The most reasonable thing to do is accept Christ.

Questions

1. To Lewis it is important that Jesus offered a perfect sacrifice of surrender and humiliation. Does it matter whether or not His sacrifice was perfect? Should it be important to you?
2. The phrase, "if we share the humility and suffering of Jesus" is at the heart of the Christian faith. What does it mean to share the humility and suffering of Jesus?
3. Notice the results of sharing the humility and suffering of Jesus. Everyone who has ever lived has had a problem with death—everyone dies. But for the Christian, death is just a transition to a new life as Lewis states. Everyone would like to be perfect and perfectly happy. Do you see that fulfillment of this desire is part of the bargain for the believer in Christ?
4. Do you understand why it is not enough just to try harder to be good; to do good? Do you understand why we have to come to the point of admitting that we can't save ourselves? Christianity is not a self-help program.
5. To me, one of the most important statements Lewis makes in the entire book is the following: "The Christian thinks that any good he does comes from the life of Christ within him. He doesn't think that God will love us because we are good, but that God will make us good because He loves us." Would you agree? Do you understand what he is saying? Explain.
6. What do you say to the person who says God is being unfair to people who have never heard of Jesus to require that they believe in Him in order to be made right with God?
7. What do you say to someone who says that God should just swoop down and eliminate evil once and for all and let us all live together in peace and happiness for ever after?

Book 3. Christian Behavior

1. The Three Parts of Morality

Preliminary Comments

Lewis starts this section by relating a story about a schoolboy who was asked what he thought God was like. He replied that as far as he could make out, God was the sort of person who is always snooping around to see if anyone is enjoying himself and then trying to stop it.

Lewis suggests that moral rules exist for specific and helpful purposes:
- Moral rules are directions for running the human machine.
- Every rule exists to prevent a failure in the operation of that machine.

Some prefer to talk about moral *ideals* rather than moral rules and about moral *idealism* rather than moral obedience. But there are problems with this approach:
- It is dangerous to describe a person who tries very hard to keep the moral law as a man of high ideals, because this might lead one to think that moral perfection was a private taste of his own and that the rest of us are not called on to share it.
- It would be even more dangerous to think of oneself as a person of high ideals because one is trying to tell no lies at all (instead of only a few lies) or never to commit adultery (instead of committing it only seldom).

Every moral failure is going to cause trouble, probably to others and certainly to yourself.

There are two ways in which the human machine goes wrong:
- When individuals drift apart or collide with one another.
- When things go wrong inside the individual.

Lewis uses the illustration of ships sailing in formation to communicate these important ideas. He says the voyage will be a success only if the ships don't get in one another's way, and if the individual ships are seaworthy.

Then he adds a third element that is necessary for the voyage to be a success: the fleet of ships obviously has to have some destination, so the objective is for all of them to get there.

Three Facets of Morality

According to his preliminary arguments, Lewis is now ready to declare that there are three concerns of morality:
- Fair play and harmony between individuals.
- Harmonizing the things inside each individual.
- The purpose of human life as a whole.

Modern people are nearly always thinking about the first thing and forgetting the other two.

When someone says about something he wants to do, "It can't be wrong because it doesn't do anyone else any harm," he is thinking only of the first thing.

It is natural, Lewis writes, when we start thinking about morality to begin with the first thing for a couple of reasons:
- The results of moral failure in that sphere are so obvious and affect us daily.
- As long as you stick to the first thing, there is very little disagreement about morality.

Almost all people in all times have agreed that human beings ought to be honest and kind and helpful to one another.

But unless we go on to the second thing, we are only deceiving ourselves.

- What good is drawing up rules for social behavior on paper if we know that our greed, cowardice, ill-temper, and self-conceit are going to prevent us keeping them?
- You cannot make men good by law (you can't legislate morality); without good men you cannot have a good society.

So we must go on to think of the second thing—morality within the individual. And here is where different beliefs about the universe lead to different behavior.

If someone thinks that a thing cannot be wrong unless it hurts another human being, we must ask further, whether it is acceptable if it hurts the individual who does the thing. One's answer to this second question depends on one's view of a Someone to whom we are accountable for our actions—even to actions that hurt only ourselves.
- If one doesn't believe in a higher power to whom one is accountable, then it really doesn't matter how he or she lives as long as no one else is hurt (difficult to imagine any behavior at all that would not affect someone other than the actor—a parent, spouse, child, etc.).
- Christians believe that Someone else created us for His own purposes, and therefore we will have many duties and responsibilities that we would not have if we simply belonged to ourselves.

Furthermore, one's view of eternity makes a very great difference in how we will behave. Christians believe that they will live forever; others have no such beliefs.
- If I believe that I will only live for seventy or so years, my bad temper might be just an occasional irritant to me and to others.
- If I believe I am going to live forever, I really need to do something about it—especially if it is getting worse with the passing of time.

46

And our view of eternity makes a very great difference in the value we place on an individual vis-à-vis the value we place on a state or a civilization.
- If we believe that people only live for seventy or so years, then a state, nation, or civilization is far more important than an individual.
- If we believe individuals live forever, then individuals are far more important than states, nations, or civilizations which are temporal.

Summary of Chapter 1

When we think about morality, we must think of three areas:
- Relations between man and man.
- Things inside each man.
- Relations between man and the power that made him.

Dealing with the third of these areas is where the main differences between Christian and non-Christian moralities come into play.

Questions

1. Do you understand why it is necessary to talk about moral rules rather than moral ideals and moral obedience rather than moral idealism? Ideals and idealism are namby-pamby words that don't really have any connection with personal responsibility. What would you say to someone who said that he had high ideals?
2. Lewis has done a wonderful thing in defining morality in terms of these three concerns. Have you ever thought about morality in these categories? Do you think you could explain these concerns to a moral relativist?
3. What would you say to someone who says that something isn't wrong if it doesn't hurt anyone? By the way, we hear this every day in modern society. For example, it doesn't matter what people do behind their bedroom door, as long as no one

else knows or pornography is OK because it only affects the one looking and no one else.

4. Do you agree that most people now who speak of morality are only concerning themselves with the first category? Can you give some examples? Do you ever excuse your own failures by only focusing on the first category?

5. Do you agree with Lewis' statement that "almost all people in all times have agreed that human beings ought to be honest and kind and helpful to one another?" What about terrorists?

6. Do you agree that we can't make men good by law? Be careful—this is a trick question. Why do we have laws that make it illegal to murder someone or to rob someone?

7. Do you understand why our view of the universe and eternity affects our view of the value of an individual? What do you say to someone who advocates a woman's right to choice or to someone who argues that it is OK to withhold sustenance from a terminally ill person?

2. The Cardinal Virtues

Introduction

Another way of looking at the whole issue of morality is that which classic writers used, but which Lewis couldn't include in his earlier radio broadcasts. According to this scheme, there are seven "virtues." Four of these are called "Cardinal Virtues" and the remaining three are called "Theological Virtues."
- Cardinal virtues are those which all civilized people recognize.
- Only Christians know about the Theological virtues.

The word *cardinal* has nothing to do with officers in the Catholic Church (or with professional baseball), it is a Latin term meaning "the hinge of a door," and in our context cardinal means these virtues are pivotal.

Prudence

Prudence means practical common sense, taking the trouble to think out what you are doing and the likely consequences of your actions. Jesus wants us to have a certain character:
- He wants a child's heart. He wants us to be simple, single-minded, affectionate, and teachable, as good children are.
- He also wants us to have a grown-up's head. He wants every bit of intelligence we have to be alert at its job, and in first-class fighting trim.

We should not be content with the same babyish ideas we had when we were young. If we are, God will not love us any less; or have less use for us, if we were born with a second-rate brain. He has room for people with little sense, but He wants everyone to use what sense they have.

The proper motto is not:
- "Be good, sweet maid, and let who can be clever." But,

- "Be good, sweet maid and don't forget that this involves being as clever as you can."

Lewis warns those who might be considering Christianity that they are embarking on something that will take their whole being— brains and all. And, fortunately, it works the other way around, anyone who is honestly trying to live as a Christian will find his intelligence being sharpened.

Temperance

Temperance refers to all pleasures, and it means not abstaining, but going the right length and no farther. Lewis laments that the word in its modern usage has come to mean abstinence from alcohol or "teetotalism." Islam, not Christianity, is the religion of total abstinence from alcohol.

Here are a couple of characteristics of temperance.
- There will be times when Christians will abstain from various things which they like to see other people enjoying, not because they condemn them, but for other valid reasons.
- One of the marks of a certain type of *bad* person is that he cannot give up a thing without wanting everyone else to give it up also. This is not a Christian attitude.

The problem with associating the term temperance only with alcohol is that it allows people to forget that it is possible to be intemperate about lots of things. Lewis mentions, as examples, golf, bridge, and pets; and he notes that being intemperate in these areas is not as noticeable as being intemperate in the use of alcohol, but God is not deceived in any case—He knows when we have gone over the line.

Justice

Lewis points out that justice is more than we think off the top of our head:

- Justice is much more than the sort of thing that goes on in the law courts. It is more than convicting and punishing evildoers.
- Justice is what we would also call "fairness." It includes honesty, give and take, truthfulness, keeping promises and the like.

Recall, in the previous chapter, Lewis wrote, "Almost all people in all times have agreed that human beings ought to be honest and kind and helpful to one another." Thus, he believes that most people have an underlying commitment to the notion of justice.

Fortitude

The closest word we have today that describes what Lewis means when he speaks of fortitude is "guts." Fortitude includes two kinds of courage:
- The kind that is willing to face danger.
- The kind that "sticks it" under pain.

It should be obvious that without fortitude, one cannot practice any of the other virtues for very long without giving up.

Conclusions

There is a difference between doing some just or temperate action and being a just or temperate man. A just or temperate man possesses a certain quality of character, and it is that quality rather than an action that we mean when we speak of the virtue.

If we only think of actions as virtues we might encourage three wrong ideas:
- We might think if one does the right thing, it doesn't matter what the motivation is. The truth is that right actions done for the wrong reason do not help to build the internal quality or character called a virtue.

- We might think that God wanted simply obedience to a set of rules; whereas He really wants people of a particular sort of character.
- We might think that the virtues were necessary only for this present life—that in the other world we would stop being just because there is nothing about which to quarrel and stop being brave because there is no danger.

Lewis concludes by suggesting that the crucial point is not that God will refuse you admission to His eternal world if you haven't got certain qualities of character; the point is that if people have not got at least the beginnings of those qualities inside them, then no possible external conditions could make a "heaven" for them—that is, could make them happy with the deep, strong, unshakeable kind of happiness God intends for us.

Summary of Chapter 2

Another way of thinking about morality is using the concept of the seven virtues: four so-called cardinal virtues and three theological virtues. The cardinal virtues are:
- Prudence. Thinking out the consequences of actions.
- Temperance. Moderation in all things.
- Justice. Fairness toward others.
- Fortitude. Facing danger and perseverance.

If people don't have the beginnings of these character attributes, they will be in trouble in the present world and absent in the next.

Questions

1. Lewis writes, "Cardinal virtues are those which all civilized people recognize." What does he mean by the term *civilized*? We typically characterize teen-agers as intemperate, but we think they are civilized. What about terrorists, who are supposed to be civilized, but are unspeakably unjust in much of what they do?

2. Did you catch what Lewis says about Christians using every measure of their intelligence? Studies suggest that 25 percent of American adults did not read a single book last year. Is this exercising one's intelligence? What is the connection between prudence and Christian maturity?
3. Would you classify yourself as a temperate person? Are there any areas in which you are intemperate? Borderline intemperate? Should one be temperate with respect to the Scriptures? With respect to one's devotion to Jesus? Can intemperance in other areas of life lead to our being less devoted to Jesus than we ought?
4. Are you always kind and considerate of others? Of waitresses? Of internationals on the roads or in stores? It is easy to be kind and fair and honest with family members and friends. It gets a little sticky when it comes down to being just with those who are different from us. Do you think Americans have an advantage in this area? ("… With liberty and *justice* for all.")
5. How would you rate your fortitude? In being willing to face danger? In being willing to see things through to appropriate conclusions? Do you see how if you don't measure up in the area of fortitude, it is tough to make the cut with the other virtues? Explain.
6. What would you say to someone who said, "Oh, Christianity is just keeping a bunch of antiquated rules?" Do you think many people today have this impression of the Christian faith? Do you ever slip into the rule keeping mode?

3. Social Morality

Introduction

Lewis now turns to what he calls social morality—or the morality between man and man. He begins by noting two important points.

- Jesus did not come to preach any brand new morality. He suggests that the Golden Rule of the New Testament—"Do as you would be done by"—is a summing up of what everyone, at bottom, has always known to be right.
- Christianity has not, and does not profess to have, a detailed program for applying the Golden Rule to a particular society at a particular moment.

Christianity was never meant to replace or supersede the ordinary human arts and sciences. It is rather a director which will set them all to the right jobs, and a source of energy which will give them all new life, put at its disposal.

When people say the church ought to lead in this regard, they would be correct only if they mean the whole body of practicing Christians. Moreover,

- Those Christians who have the right talents—economists and statesmen—should direct their entire efforts in the political arena to putting the Golden Rule into action.
- And all the rest of us should follow their lead and seek to implement the Golden Rule in our own areas of endeavor.

If this were done, Lewis maintains, we would find solutions to our social ills quickly. So he suggests that the application of Christian principles is fundamentally the job of Christian laymen, not that of religious leaders.

A Christian Society

The New Testament, without going into details, gives us a pretty clear hint of what a fully Christian society would be like:

- There would be no passengers and no parasites; if a man does not work, he does not eat.
- Everyone is to work with his own hands; everyone's work is to produce something good. There would be no silly luxuries, nor advertising to entice.
- There is to be no "swank" or "side"—putting on airs. Lewis characterizes such a society as "Leftist."
- It would always be insisting on obedience—obedience (and outward signs of respect) to properly elected officials, from children to parents, and from wives to husbands.
- It would be a cheerful society: full of singing and rejoicing and regarding worry or anxiety as wrong.
- It would be a courteous society, and one absent of gossip or "busybodies."

If such a society were in existence, and we visited it, we might have varying impressions:
- We might feel that its economic life was very socialistic— Lewis says, "advanced."
- We might think its family life and its code of manners were rather old-fashioned.

Each of us would like some elements of it, but Lewis suspects that few of us would like the whole thing. And this is exactly why, according to Lewis, we never get any closer to an ideal society, because we can't agree even though we all say we are striving for a Christian society.

Lewis suggests that there are two ways to understand the Biblical prohibitions of charging interest.
- Three great civilizations (Israel, Greece, and Europe) agreed in condemning the capitalistic economic system. Lewis admits that he may have misunderstood economic history and he would be glad to defer this to Christian economists.
- Some say that when Moses, Aristotle, and Christian teachers of the Middle Ages, told us not to lend money at interest (usury)

they could not foresee the joint stock company and were only thinking of private money-lenders.

Charity

Lewis points out that charity—giving to the poor—is an essential part of Christian morality. He dismisses as an excuse the notion that instead of giving to the poor we ought to be trying to create a society in which there are no poor.

He then addresses the issue of "how much one ought to give to charity" and he concludes that we can't really settle on specifics here. He does propose some guidelines:

- We should give more than we can spare. That is, if our expenditures on comforts, luxuries, amusements, etc. are commensurate with those of others in our income class, we are probably giving too little. If our charities don't pinch or hamper us they are too small.
- Particular cases of distress among relatives, friends, neighbors, or employees, which God may bring to our attention, may demand much more—even to the crippling or endangering of our own position.

Lewis suggests two obstacles to giving:

- Fear of insecurity rather than luxurious living.
- Pride manifested in showy forms of generosity.

He points out that Leftists might think he has not gone far enough with all of this, while most (of us) might think he has gone too far.

Conclusions

A Christian society is not going to arrive until most of us really want it; and we are not going to want it until we are fully Christian. Lewis thinks there is a natural progression in play here:

- We can't carry out the Golden Rule, until we love our neighbor as we love ourselves.

- We can't love our neighbor as we love ourselves until we learn to love God as we ought.
- We can't love God as we ought until we learn to obey Him.

So before we can look outward to our relationships with others, we must look inward to our relationship with God.

Summary of Chapter 3

Here are the essential characteristics of a Christian society as Lewis describes it:
- Productive.
- Spartan.
- Forthright.
- Obedient and respectful.
- Cheerful and joyful.
- Courteous.

We might not like every aspect of such a society if indeed it existed.

Questions

1. Lewis tells us that Jesus did not come to bring a "brand new" morality. He says that people have always known what is right; that the Golden Rule is the best summary of right conduct we have, and that we just need to obey what we already know. Would you agree or disagree with his assessment? Remember, he is talking about social interactions only, not personal salvation.
2. Lewis doesn't want pastors and bishops building "Christian houses" or writing "Christian literature." He wants lay people applying Christian principles in their respective disciplines. How does this affect you? Have you ever thought about how your Christian faith should affect the practice of your professional or work life?

3. We are living in a society that is becoming crass and self-indulgent. Personally, I find much in today's world which bothers me. What about you? Do you think the kind of society Lewis has set before us as a Christian society might be a refreshing change to what we are experiencing now? How do we move away from where we are and toward what he is describing?

4. I don't suspect many of us would come down on the side of Lewis with regard to lending money at interest. Given that the notion of "interest" is a foundational aspect of our capitalistic system, do you see any applications of Christian principles in modern-day American capitalism that we ought to observe?

5. Lewis suggests that a Christian society is not going to arrive until most of us really want it and we are not going to want it until we become fully Christian. Billy Graham often said that only about 5 percent of Christians were "spiritually mature." That doesn't portend too well for the appearance of a Christian society. What are we to do?

6. We know that heaven will be a perfect representation of a Christian society. Jesus will be universally honored, and we will all be transformed into His likeness, we will possess the character of Christ. Do you suppose there will be any aspects of heaven that we won't like? Why or why not?

4. Morality and Psychoanalysis

Introduction

Lewis returns to a comment he made in the previous chapter to enlarge on it. He wrote, "we should never get a Christian society unless most of us became Christian individuals." That doesn't mean that we can put off doing anything about society until some imaginary future date when it will be marvelously transformed. He says we must begin two tasks at once:

- The job of how the Golden Rule can be applied in detail to modern society.
- The job of becoming the sort of people who would apply it if we saw how.

This leads Lewis to consider the Christian idea of a good man—the Christian specification for the human machine, as he puts it.

Christianity and Psychoanalysis

Since Christianity claims to be an approach for putting the human machine right, Lewis wants to contrast it with another approach which makes the same claims—psychoanalysis. Lewis believed that when Freud was talking about curing neurotics, he was speaking as an expert, but when he wandered into philosophy, he was an amateur. Lewis writes that pure psychoanalysis (without all the additions made by Freud and others) is not in the least contradictory to Christianity.

According to Lewis, when someone makes a moral choice there are two things involved:

- One thing is the act of choosing.
- The other is the various feelings, impulses and so on which his psychological makeup presents him with, and which are the raw material of his choice. The raw material Lewis says may be of two kinds:

- Normal—the kind of feelings that are common to all men. For example,
    - The fear of dangerous things.
    - The desire of a man for a woman.
- Unnatural—feelings due to things that have gone wrong in his subconscious. For example,
    - The irrational fear of harmless things.
    - The perverted desire of a man for a woman.

Psychoanalysis undertakes to remove abnormal feelings, that is, to give the individual better raw material for his acts of choice. Morality is concerned with the acts of choice.

And Lewis gives an example of three men who go to war to illustrate:
- The first man:
    - Has a natural fear of dangerous things.
    - He subdues it by moral effort, that is:
        - He chooses his sense of patriotism over
        - His fear of danger posed by battle.
    - He becomes a brave man.
- The second man.
    - Has an exaggerated, irrational fear of danger.
    - No amount of moral effort can overcome his fear.
    - A psychologist is able to cure the man's fear.
    - He is able to perform admirably under fire because:
        - He chooses his sense of patriotism over
        - His fear of danger posed by battle.
- The third man.
    - Has an exaggerated, irrational fear of danger.
    - No amount of moral effort can overcome his fear.
    - A psychologist is able to cure the man's fear.
    - He is shirks his duty under fire because:
        - He chooses to look out for Number One over
        - His sense of patriotism.

The difference between the first two men is moot; the difference between the second two is purely a moral choice, based the facts of the decision. Morality is concerned only with free choices; the second two men are identical to the first man with respect to the choices before them.

The bad psychological material is not a sin to be repented of, but a disease to be cured. Humans judge one another by our external actions, but God judges by moral choices. Lewis gives two illustrations:
- A neurotic with a pathological fear of cats might pick up a kitten to remove it from a roadway. In God's eyes, he might have shown more courage that a normal person who won the Medal of Honor.
- A man who has been perverted from his youth and taught that cruelty is right might do some simple kindness for another. In God's eyes, he could be doing more than one who gives up his life for a friend.

This is why Christians are told not to judge (condemn). We only see the results which a man's choices make out of his raw material. God does not judge him on the raw material at all, but on what he has done with it.

Christian Morality

Lewis suggests that there are two very different ways of thinking about Christian morality:
- A bargain in which God says, "if you'll keep a lot of rules, I'll reward you, and if you don't I'll punish you."
- Every time you make a moral choice, you are turning the central part of yourself, the part that chooses, into something different:
  - Either into a heavenly creature in harmony with God and other creatures and with itself. To be this kind of creature is joy and peace and knowledge and power.

- Or into a creature that is in a state of war with God and its fellow creatures and with itself. To be this kind of creature means madness, horror, idiocy, rage, impotence, and eternal loneliness.

Lewis says that this latter view explains something that used to puzzle him about Christian writers:
- They seemed to be very strict one moment when they wrote about sins of thought that were immensely important.
- They seemed very free the next moment when they discussed terrible murders and other treacheries as though all one had to do was repent and all would be forgiven.

And Lewis thinks they were right because they were thinking of the mark which the action leaves on the soul that no one sees in this life but which we will have to endure—or enjoy—forever. The bigness or smallness of the thing is not what matters, but that we have done something to ourselves which, unless we repent, will make it more difficult to withstand the next time we are tempted along those lines.

Lewis concludes by observing that the right direction leads not only to peace but to knowledge.
- When a man is getting better, he understands more and more clearly the evil that is still left in him. A moderately bad man knows he is not very good.
- When a man is getting worse, he understands his own badness less and less. A thoroughly bad man thinks he is all right.

Good people know about both good and evil; bad people do not know about either.

Summary of Chapter 4

Lewis contrasts Christian moral choices with psychoanalysis and shows that there is nothing incompatible with these two approaches.

He says there are two very different views of Christian morality.

- Rule keeping with rewards or consequences.
- Making moral choices that either enhance or degrade our character.

Making the correct moral choices leads to peace and knowledge.

Questions

1. If you are like me, you were a little put off by Lewis addressing the connection between Christian morality and psychoanalysis. Yet after reading his explanation, I found myself agreeing with him. Do you believe there is a place for psychologists in treating fears and phobias?

2. Lewis writes that irrational fears are not sins for which one seeks forgiveness, but diseases for which one seeks a cure. Is this correct? What, then, is the difference between an irrational fear of danger, and an uncontrollable desire for alcohol or drugs? Do you see the very important point Lewis is making here? It may be more difficult for those of us with relatively normal psyches than for those with problems in this area.

3. The most frequently quoted Bible verse in our post-modern culture is Matthew 7:1, "Do not judge lest you be judged yourselves." Here Jesus is speaking of condemnation rather than discrimination. We are certainly expected to exercise judgment when observing the behavior of others. Do you understand the distinction? Can you explain it?

4. Suppose you saw someone you cared for engaging in destructive behavior. What would be the appropriate Christian response? To ignore it because it would cause you to appear judgmental, or to confront them, in love, and try to persuade them to address the situation?

5. Don't you love the contrast Lewis makes between rule keeping and making moral choices? When I think of moral choices marking my soul and either making it easier or more difficult to overcome a temptation the next time, it impresses me to be about making the right choices all the time. What about you?

6. Do you agree with Lewis that making correct moral choices leads not only to peace but to knowledge? Do you think there are people who make wrong moral choices who also have peace? What about people who make wrong moral choices who have heightened moral insight?

5. Sexual Morality

Introduction

Lewis now considers Christian morality as regards sex or what Christians refer to as the virtue of chastity. He warns that we must not confuse chastity with modesty (propriety or decency):

- Chastity as a Christian virtue is either marriage with complete faithfulness to your partner or total abstinence.
  - The rule of chastity is the same for all Christians in all times.
  - Chastity is probably the most unpopular of the Christian virtues.
- Propriety is a social rule which prescribes how much of the human body may be displayed and what subjects may be referred to and in what words.
  - The standards of propriety change from society to society and from time to time.
  - When people break the rule of propriety, we must consider the motivation:
    - If they do so in order to excite lust in themselves or others, they are offending against chastity.
    - If they break it defiantly in order to shock or embarrass others, they are being uncharitable (but not necessarily unchaste).
    - If they do so through ignorance or carelessness, they are only guilty of bad manners.

Lewis himself was in favor of a somewhat relaxed notion of propriety (vis-à-vis that of Victorian England). He acknowledged that in its present form propriety has the inconvenience that people of different ages and types do not all observe the same standard. He suggests:

- That old or old-fashioned people be very careful not to assume that younger or "emancipated" people are corrupt whenever they exceed the older standard.

- That younger people should not call their elders "prudes" or "puritans" because they do not easily adapt to the new standard.

He thought that a real desire to believe all the good you can of others and to make others as comfortable as you can, would solve most of the problems in this area.

Sexual Instincts

Lewis suggests that Christian chastity is so different and so contrary to our instincts that either Christianity is wrong or our sexual instinct, as it is now, has gone wrong. Of course, as a Christian, he believes our sexual instinct is the problem, and he gives three reasons for thinking so.
- First, he considers biological function, and he compares eating and sex to make his point.
    - The biological purpose of eating is to repair the body. He notes that the appetite for food goes a little beyond its biological function, but not enormously.
    - The biological purpose of sex is to reproduce. Lewis maintains that our appetite for sex is in ludicrous and preposterous excess of its function.
- A second way of proving the point is to compare our interest in (or preoccupation with) food and sex.
    - He suggests that if we lived in a country where people went to theaters to view plates of food unveiled, we would conclude they were either:
        - Starving. There was no food to be had and one could only look.
        - Perverted. There was something exaggerated about their interest in food.
    - Since we live in countries where people engage in various forms of sexual voyeurism (movies, magazines, TV, Internet, etc.), we must conclude we are either:
        - Starving. Severe sexual abstinence in society.

- Perverted. There was something exaggerated about our interest in sex.

  Lewis suggests that there is no evidence that there is more sexual abstinence in our own age than in past ages. He observes that contraceptives have made sexual indulgence lest costly within marriage and far safer outside marriage than ever before, and public opinion less hostile to illicit unions than since Pagan times. Thus he concludes that on the basis of preoccupation, it appears that our sexual instinct is exaggerated.
- A third way is to consider existing perversions of eating and perversions of sexual behavior.
  - Very few people want to eat things that are really not food or to do other things with food instead of eating it.
  - Perversions of the sex instinct are numerous, difficult to cure, and offend even the most hardened sensibilities.

Lewis identifies several lies we have been fed about the sexual instinct:
- "Sex has become a mess because it was hushed up. If we only abandon this Victorian idea, everything will be OK."
  - It has been out in the open for a generation, and it is not OK.
  - Lewis believes that the reason it was hushed up to begin with was because it was a problem.
- "Sex is nothing to be ashamed of." There are two different ways this can be taken; it is correct in one sense and not in the other.
  - "There is nothing to be ashamed of in the fact that the human race reproduces itself in a certain way, nor in the fact that it gives pleasure." This is correct.
    - Christianity certainly affirms this view. Some think that if man had never fallen, sexual pleasure would have been greater.
    - Christianity thoroughly approves the body.
      - Matter is good, thus our bodies are good.
      - God Himself took on a human body.

67

- □ We will have glorified bodies in heaven.
  - Christianity glorifies marriage.
- "The state into which the sexual instinct has gotten is nothing to be ashamed of." This is wrong.
  - There is nothing to be ashamed of in enjoying your food; if half the world made food the main interest of their lives and spent their time looking at pictures of food and dribbling and smacking their lips, something is wrong!
  - Our ancestors have handed over to us organisms which are warped in this respect.
    - □ We grow up surrounded by propaganda in favor of un-chastity.
    - □ There are people who want to keep our sex instinct inflamed in order to make money from us.
  - God knows our situation; He will not judge us as though we had no difficulties to overcome. What matters is our sincerity and perseverance to overcome them.

Sexual Chastity

Lewis suggests that there are three reasons why it is especially difficult for us to desire—let alone achieve—complete chastity:
- Our warped natures, those who tempt us, and the contemporary propaganda combine to make us feel that the desires we are restraining are "natural," "healthy," and "reasonable;" that it is almost perverse and abnormal to resist them.
  - The lie here is that any sexual act to which one is tempted is healthy and normal.
  - Every sane and civilized individual has some set of principles by which he chooses to reject some of his desires and permit others.
- Many people are deterred from seriously attempting Christian chastity because they think, before trying, that it is impossible. When a thing has to be attempted, one must never think about the possibility or impossibility.
  - We must ask for God's help.

- God may give us the desire to try before we succeed with the virtue.
- Trying cures our illusions about ourselves.
- People misunderstand what psychology teaches about "repression." It teaches that repressed sex is dangerous.
  - Repressed does not mean denied or resisted.
  - Repressed does mean being forced into the subconscious.

Lewis closes his discussion on sexual morality by showing that it is not the center of Christian morality. The sins of the flesh are bad, he says, but they are the least bad of all sins.
- The Animal Self, those physical sins which compete with the human self I am trying to become; adultery, promiscuity, sex outside of marriage, homosexual sex, are not the worst sins.
- The Diabolical Self, those spiritual sins are the ones which may destroy my soul; anger, pride, hatred, self-centeredness, these are the ones no one sees, which eat away at my personhood.

Summary of Chapter 5

- Lewis distinguishes between social propriety and Christian chastity.
- He offers proof that the sexual instinct in men has gone wrong.
- He explains why achieving complete Christian chastity is so difficult.

Questions

1. Lewis has done a wonderful thing for us in distinguishing between chastity and propriety. Chastity is an absolute standard—it never changes. Propriety, on the other hand, changes with societies and with time. Can you give some examples of acceptable changes in propriety that have occurred in our lifetime?
2. Do you understand the tension between the generations where propriety or modesty is concerned? Can you recall coming into conflict with others in this area? Your parents? Your

children? Lewis' remedy for most such conflicts is having "a real desire to believe all the good you can of others and to make others as comfortable as you can." He believes this would solve most of the problems in this area. Can you think of instances where this approach would be inappropriate?

3. Comparing our eating habits with our sexual behavior is a clever way of demonstrating that there is something amiss with our sexual instincts. Do you accept his arguments as plausible? Do you think many Americans in the 21st century would agree with Lewis?

4. Have we really been fed a pack of lies about sexual behavior? Do you think many of our contemporaries have bought into the lies? Do you see how some of these very things are fundamental to our West-East cultural divide today? Can you explain?

5. Is the notion of complete chastity so out-of-line with our culture and with our sexual appetites, that we ought to scrap it altogether? Be very careful with your answer here, because if you do decide that chastity ought to be junked, you will need to substitute some other sexual standard in its place. Like the guy who wrote to my hometown newspaper and said he thought we ought to forget the commandment about adultery. What would you offer in the place of chastity?

6. Do you agree with Lewis that sexual behavior is not at the center of Christian morality? Why are offenses of our Diabolical Self far more serious than those of our Animal Self? Do you agree that we are under constant warfare to restrain the appetites of our Diabolical Self, and that it is only with God's help that we can succeed in this regard? (see Romans 7:15-25)

6. Christian Marriage

Introduction

Lewis states at the outset two reasons why he does not particularly want to deal with Christian marriage:
- Christian doctrines on the subject are extremely unpopular.
- Having never been married, he can only speak second-hand.

He begins by observing that the Christian idea of marriage is based on Christ's words that a man and wife are to be regarded as a single organism. Christians believe that when Jesus said this:
- He was not stating a sentiment; as the inventor of the human machine, He was stating a fact regarding its operation.
- He was saying that in marriage the individuals are to be combined together, not just sexually, but totally combined.

The Christian attitude toward sexual pleasure implies:
- That there is nothing wrong about sexual pleasure anymore than there is anything wrong with eating.
- One must not isolate that pleasure and try to get it by itself anymore than trying to get pleasure from eating without swallowing.

The Christian teaching on marriage, pure and simple, is: marriage is for life. Churches differ with regard to their view of marriage—some churches permit divorce reluctantly in very special cases, others do not permit it at all.

But most churches agree about marriage in some very fundamental respects:
- They all regard divorce as something like cutting up a living body, as something like a surgical operation.
- Some of them think the operation is so violent that it cannot be done at all; others admit it as a remedy in extreme cases.
- They would all agree that it is more like amputating your legs than dissolving a business partnership.

71

They all disagree with the modern view that it is a simple readjustment of partners to be made whenever people feel they are no longer in love with one another, or when either of them falls in love with someone else.

Marriage and Justice

Lewis suggests that the Christian virtue of justice is fundamental to the idea of marriage. Justice includes the keeping of promises. Here is how justice relates to marriage:
- Everyone who has been married in a Christian ceremony has made a public, solemn promise to stick with his or her partner until death.
- The duty of keeping the marriage promise is just as it is with any other promise. And it has no special connection with the sexual impulse.
  - If the sexual impulse is like all of our other impulses, then its indulgence is controlled by our promises as are other impulses.
  - If the sexual impulse is inflamed as he has argued, then we must be especially careful not to let it lead us into dishonesty.

If someone protests that he regarded the promise as a mere formality and never intended to keep it, we must ask whom he was trying to deceive when he made the promise:
- God? That was very unwise.
- Himself? Not much wiser.
- His partner or in-laws? That was treacherous.
- The public? That is cheating. He wanted the respectability that is attached to marriage without paying the price.
  - If he is contented, Lewis has nothing more to say. He won't urge the high and hard duty of chastity on someone who hasn't wished to be merely honest.
  - If he has come to his senses and wants to be honest, his promise constrains him, and this comes under the heading of justice, not chastity.

If people do not believe in permanent marriage, it is perhaps better that they live together unmarried than making vows they don't intend to keep. Unchastity is not improved by adding perjury.

Love and Marriage

The idea that "being in love" is the only reason for remaining married really leaves no room for marriage as a contract or promise at all.

- The Christian rule is not forcing upon the passion of love something which is foreign to that passion's own nature. Those who are in love have a natural inclination to bind themselves by promises.
- The promise commits one to being true even if he ceases to be in love. A promise must be made about things one can fulfill, about actions; no one can promise to go on feeling a certain way.

We might ask, what is the use of keeping two people together if they are no longer in love. There are two very good reasons.

- To provide a home for the children if there are any.
- To protect the woman who usually has sacrificed for the marriage.

Lewis now probes into the meaning of the phrase "being in love." He maintains that being in love is a glorious state and good for us in several ways.

- It helps make us generous and courageous.
- It opens our eyes to beauty—that of the beloved and all beauty.
- It subordinates our merely animal sexuality, especially at first.

Lewis repeats a statement he made earlier: "the most dangerous thing you can do is to take any of your impulses and set it up as the thing you ought to follow at all costs."

- Being in love is a good thing, but it is not the best thing.
- There are things below it, but there are also things above it.
- You cannot make it the basis of a whole life.

Love as distinct from "being in love" is not merely a feeling.

- It is a deep unity, maintained by the will and deliberately strengthened by habit.
- It is reinforced (in Christian marriages) by the grace both partners ask and receive from God.
- They can have this love for each other even in moments when they do not like each other.
- They can retain this love even when each would easily, if they allowed themselves, "be in love" with someone else.

"Being in love" first moved them to promise fidelity; this quieter love enables them to keep the promise. It is on this love that the engine of marriage is run; being in love was the explosion that started it.

Our experience is thoroughly colored by the media—books, movies, television. We have to disentangle the things we have heard from real life.

- People have the idea that if you have married the "right" person, you may expect to go on being in love forever.
- Consequently, when the glamour has gone out of the relationship, they think they have made a mistake and are entitled to a change.
- And, of course, when the change has been made the glamour will go out of the new love just as it went out of the old.

Lewis now addresses what we might call mature love. He writes that in the area of love, as in every other, thrills come at the beginning and do not last. He says that we gain by persevering through the dying of the thrills.

- The dying away of the first thrill will be compensated by a quieter, more lasting, kind of interest.
- People who are ready to submit to the loss of the thrill and settle down to the sober interest will likely meet new thrills in some different direction.

- Let the thrill go—let it die away—go on through that period of death into the quieter interest and happiness will follow.

If you decide to make thrills your regular diet and try to prolong them artificially, they will get weaker and weaker, and fewer and fewer, and you will be a bored, disillusioned old man for the rest of your life.

Another notion we get from the media is that "falling in love" is something quite irresistible; something that just happens to one.
- Because they believe this, some married people throw in the sponge and give up when they find themselves attracted by a new acquaintance.
- It is largely in our own choice whether this love shall, or shall not, turn into what we call being in love.
- If our minds are full of movies and sentimental songs and our bodies full of alcohol, we can turn every love we feel into this kind of love.

Other Issues

Lewis concludes by considering two issues which we often confuse. The first is the issue of how far Christians ought to go in trying to force their views of marriage on society as a whole.
- He wishes that the government would recognize that the majority of British people are not Christians and, therefore, cannot be expected to live Christian lives.
- His solution would be to have two distinct kinds of marriages: one governed by the state with rules enforced on all citizens, the other governed by the church with rules enforced by her on her own members.

He suggests the distinction ought to be quite sharp, so that we would know the difference between a state marriage and a Christian one.

Now Lewis turns to the role of the partners in Christian marriages—an issue that he correctly characterizes as very unpopular. Christian wives promise to obey their husbands and the husband in a Christian marriage is to be the "head." There are two facets of this issue:

- Why should there be a head at all—why not equality? Lewis' answer to this first question is that in a permanent union of two people, in case of disagreement, someone has to be able to cast the deciding vote.
- If there must be a head, why should it be the man? Lewis offers two different reasons why he thinks the husband should be the head in a Christian marriage.
    - Lewis thought there was something unnatural about the rule of wives over husbands, because "wives themselves are half ashamed of it and despise the husbands whom they rule."
    - The relations of the family to the outer world—what might be called its foreign policy—must depend, in the last resort, on the man, because he always ought to be, and usually is, much more just to outsiders.

Summary of Chapter 6

- Let Christian teaching on marriage, pure and simple, is: marriage is for life.
- Lewis suggests that the Christian virtue of justice is fundamental to the idea of marriage. Justice includes the keeping of promises.
- He explains "love" is distinct from "being in love." And he discusses how we are to cultivate "mature love."
- Finally, he deals with two controversial issues: why there must be a "head" in the marriage relationship, and why the man is the head.

Questions

1. For someone who was not married when he wrote this, Lewis has a remarkable grasp on what Christian marriage ought to be. What did you think of his presentation, having read it? I have already recommended the chapter to friends whose adult son is struggling with some of these issues. Can you think of anyone who would benefit from reading this chapter?

2. Lewis sees the Christian virtue of justice—that is, keeping promises—as fundamental to marriage. This is certainly a message that the present generation really needs to hear. Would you agree? How important do you believe keeping promises and commitments is in living Christianly in today's world?

3. In this chapter are four attributes Lewis uses to distinguish "love" from "being in love." Reread these attributes and discuss them individually in your group. These are too profound to gloss over. Do you see these attributes at work in your own marriage?

4. Do you believe that our attitudes are deeply affected by the media? Even though many of us have been following Jesus for years, we can still be impacted by the lure of the media. What are some ways we can keep from being influenced by incorrect ideas that are continually presented in the media?

5. Do you know someone who has "fallen in love" with someone, not his wife, and walked out on a good wife and good marriage? What advice do you have for such a person after having read Lewis' chapter on Christian Marriage?

6. Do you agree with Lewis that as Christians we ought not to impose our ideals on those in our society who are not Christians? Is there anywhere that we must draw a line and say as the Australian Prime Minister did recently, "This is what we practice here, either comply or leave?"

7. Why are the issues of submission and headship so controversial?

7. Forgiveness

Forgiveness in Theory

Lewis begins his discussion of forgiveness by saying that he had suggested earlier that chastity was the most unpopular of the Christian virtues. He now says he thinks it might be forgiveness.

Forgiveness is established as a virtue by the admonition to "Love your neighbor as yourself." And the principle is extended by Jesus in the Sermon on the Mount to include the "terrible duty of forgiving our enemies."

Lewis writes that everyone thinks the notion of forgiveness is a lovely idea in principle, until one has someone to forgive, and then it is met by howls of anger.
- It is not that people think it too high and difficult.
- But that people think it hateful and contemptible.

They might ask, "How would you feel forgiving the Gestapo if you were a Pole or a Jew?"

Lewis underscores that he is not telling in the book what he would do, but he is trying to explain what Christianity is—what Christian behavior is. He restates the principle from what we call the Lord's Prayer, "Forgive us our sins as we forgive those who sin against us." He rightly infers from this two axioms of forgiveness.
- We are offered forgiveness on no other terms.
- If we do not forgive, we will not be forgiven.

Since this is such a difficult thing for most of us to do, Lewis offers two suggestions for making forgiveness easier:
- One might begin by forgiving someone whom he or she loves for some recent offense.
- We might try to understand exactly what loving your neighbor as yourself really means.

And he offers some insights to make the task more acceptable:
- It does not mean "feel fond of him" or "find him attractive."
- Neither does it mean thinking them "nice." Lewis offers that in his clearest moments he knows that he is not a nice man; he is a very nasty one.

So we may at once loathe and hate the things our enemies do. We are to hate the sin, but not the sinner.

Lewis realized that there is one particular man he had been treating this way all of his life—himself.
- However much he disliked his own cowardice or conceit or greed, he went on loving himself.
- The very reason he hated those bad things was because he loved the man who did them.
- Because he loved himself, he was sorry to find that he was the sort of man who did those things.

Christianity wants us to hate cruelty and treachery and all such evils. But it wants us to hate them in the same way we hate them in ourselves: being sorry that the man should have done them and hoping that somehow, sometime he can be cured and made human again.

Forgiveness in Action

Lewis gives an example to make sure we understand the concepts. Suppose you read a newspaper account of some terrible atrocities; then later you read that the story might not have been quite true or that it was not as bad as it appeared. What is your reaction upon learning the truth?
- Thank God. They aren't quite as bad as that.
- Or disappointment and a determination to cling to the original story for the pleasure of thinking your enemies as bad as possible.

If it is the second, Lewis surmises that it is the first step of a process that will lead us into a universe of pure hatred.

Now, Lewis asks, "Does loving your enemy mean not punishing him?" And the answer is "No;" since we ought to subject ourselves to punishment when we are guilty of offenses; even to death.

Lewis scoffs at those who would protest against capital punishment by quoting the commandment, "Thou shalt not kill." He notes that there are actually two Greek words that are confused:
- The one (*anthropoktonos*) means "to kill."
- The other (*phoneuo*) means "to murder."

When Jesus quotes the commandment He uses the word for murder in all three Gospel accounts, Matthew, Mark, and Luke. When we execute criminals, we kill them, we don't murder them. When we kill enemies in battle, we kill them, we don't murder them. Thus there is no Biblical prohibition against killing criminals deserving of death or enemies in legitimate [just] battle.

Lewis could not understand the "semi-pacifism" which gives people the idea that if they have to fight, it ought to be done with a long face and as if you were ashamed of it.

This, then, leads to the question, "If one is allowed to condemn the enemy's acts, and punish him and kill him, what difference is left between Christian morality and the ordinary view?"
- Christians believe that individuals live forever. So what really matters is those little marks or twists on the central, inside part of the soul which are going to turn it, in the long run, into a heavenly or hellish creature.
- We may punish if necessary, but we must not enjoy it. Something inside us, the feeling of resentment, the desire to get even, must be killed.
- Even while we kill and punish we must try to feel about the enemy as we feel about ourselves—to wish that he were not

bad, to hope that in this world, or another, he may be cured, to wish his good.

This is what the Bible means to love him—to wish him good, not feeling fond of him nor saying he is nice when he is not. This means loving people who have nothing lovable about them.

We love ourselves, Lewis says, not because there is anything lovable about us, but simply because it is ourself. God intends for us to love others in the same way. And it should be easier to recall that that is how He loves us. Not for any nice, attractive qualities we think we have, but just because we are humans.

Summary of Chapter 7

- Lewis admits that forgiveness may be, after all, the most unpopular of the virtues.
- Lewis suggests the we must forgive others in the same way we forgive ourselves—not that we don't detest the wrong that they do— but that we desire good for them in love.
- He suggests that it is not wrong to punish evildoers in the same way that we ought to insist that we are punished when we do wrong.
- Finally, he deals with the difference between killing and murder; the former being justified in punishing criminals and in battle, the latter always condemned.

Questions

1. Terrorists are probably our modern day equivalent to the Nazis of Lewis' day. Have you thought at all about forgiving the 9-11 terrorists? In all probability they have gone to a Godless eternity, so your forgiveness won't help them in any way. So why bother?
2. Do you understand that God will not forgive your sins if you are unwilling to forgive the sins of those who have offended you? What does this communicate about harboring grudges or

bad feelings toward someone who has done you wrong in the past?

3. Does it help to know that you don't have to "like" those who offend you but you do have to love them? You may properly characterize them as "evil people," but you must not hate them. You may even seek to have your enemies punished and it is not wrong to want to see justice served. What is wrong is to enjoy seeing them punished.

4. When Saddam Hussein was hanged a few months ago, were you happy that he was executed? Or were you satisfied that justice was served, and sorry that an individual can be so badly mistaken about power and position?

5. Do you see that how we treat ourselves is a powerful model of how we ought to treat others? We usually detest bad things that we think or do, but we still love ourselves. How can you remind yourself when dealing with others that you should love them as you love yourself?

6. Aren't you glad that God doesn't deal with us as we deserve, but He loves us in spite of our sinful selves? Do you see that as Christians we need to give others the same grace that God gives us?

8. The Great Sin

Pride or Self-Conceit

Lewis believed that on the issue of Pride, Christian morals differ most sharply from all other moral systems. He reminds us that when he was discussing sexual morality, he suggested that that was not the center of Christian morals—Pride is the essential vice, the utmost evil.

According to Lewis, Pride manifests itself in unusual ways.
- It is the one vice of which no man or woman in the world is free.
- Hardly any person, other than a Christian, imagines they are guilty themselves.
- Hardly anyone, other than a Christian, shows any mercy toward the vice in others.
- There is no fault that makes a man more unpopular, and no fault of which we are more unconscious in ourselves.
- It was through Pride that the devil became the devil.
- Pride leads to every other vice; it is the complete anti-God state of mind.

Pride is essentially competitive—it is competitive by its very nature—while other vices are only competitive by accident.
- Each person's pride is in competition with everyone else's pride.
- Pride gets no pleasure out of having something, only having more of it than the next man.
- It is the comparison that makes one proud; the pleasure of being above the rest.

As he has stated, Pride is competitive in a way that the other vices are not. Lewis gives a couple of examples:
- The sexual impulse may drive two men into competition if they both love the same woman. But that is accidental—they could have easily liked two different women. On the other hand, the

proud man will try to win the lady, not because he wants her, but to prove that he is a better man than you.

- Greed may drive men into competition, especially for some scarce resource. The proud man, even when he has more of the resource in question than he can possibly want, will try to get still more just to assert his power.

And power is what Pride really enjoys; there is nothing which makes a man feel so superior to others than being able to control them as toy soldiers.

Pride is insatiable. If I am a proud man, then as long as there is one man in the whole world more powerful, or richer, or cleverer than I, he is my rival and my enemy.

Pride always means enmity—it is enmity.
- Enmity between man and man.
- Enmity between man and God.

In God one encounters something which is immeasurably superior to oneself.
- Unless you know God as that—and, therefore, know yourself as nothing in comparison—you do not know God at all.
- As long as you are proud, you cannot know God. A proud man is always looking down, and, thus, cannot see God at all.

This raises a terrible question. How is it that people who are quite obviously eaten up with Pride can say that they believe in God and appear to themselves very religious?
- They are worshipping an imaginary God. Theoretically they admit to be nothing before this phantom God, but imagine how he approves of them and thinks them far better than ordinary people.
- Lewis thinks this paying a penny's worth of imaginary humility toward their god and getting a dollar's worth of Pride toward their fellow man.

84

Lewis suggests that we have an effective test to detect Pride in ourselves.

- Whenever we find that our spiritual life is making us feel that we are good—above all, that we are better than someone else—we may be sure we are being acted on, not by God, but by the devil.
- The real test of being in the presence of God is that you either forget about yourself altogether, or see yourself as a small dirty object. It is better to forget about yourself altogether.

It is a terrible thing that the worst of all vices can smuggle itself into the very center of our spiritual life. How?

- The other, less serious vices, come from the devil working on us through our animal nature.
- But Pride does not come through our animal nature at all. It is purely spiritual; consequently, it is far more subtle and deadly.

Pride can often be used to beat down the simpler vices. For example:

- A teacher may appeal to a student's Pride (self-respect) to behave decently.
- A man may overcome cowardice, lust, or anger by considering them beneath his dignity.

The devil laughs at this. He is happy to see us becoming chaste, or brave, or self-controlled provided, at the same time, he is setting us up for the Dictatorship of Pride. Pride is spiritual cancer that eats up the very possibility of love, or contentment, or common sense.

Some Misunderstandings

Lewis wants to guard against four possible misunderstandings:
1. Pleasure in being praised is not Pride. The trouble begins when you pass from thinking, "I have pleased him, all is well," to thinking, "What a fine person I must be to have done this."
   - The more you delight in yourself and the less you delight in the praise, the worse you are becoming. When you delight

wholly in yourself and do not care about the praise at all, you have reached the bottom.

- This is why vanity, though it is the sort of Pride which shows most on the surface, is really the least bad and most pardonable sort. The vain person wants praise, applause, admiration, too much and is always angling for it.
- Vanity is a fault, but a childlike and even (in an odd way) a humble fault. It shows you are not yet completely contented with your own admiration. You value other people enough to want them to notice you.
- The real black, diabolical Pride comes when you look down on others so much that you don't care what they think of you. The proud man says, "Why should I care for the applause of that rabble as if what they thought was anything?"
- Thus, we must try not to be vain, but we must never call in our Pride to cure our vanity.

2. Being proud of a son, or school, or military action may or may not be sinful. If "being proud of" means "having a warm-hearted admiration for" such admiration is very far from being a sin. But if the person "puts on airs" or "affectations" this is wrong, but better than being prideful of oneself.
   - To love and admire anything outside oneself is not the issue.
   - To love or admire anything (including ourselves) more than we love and admire God is the problem.

3. We must not think Pride is something God forbids because He is offended at it, or that Humility is something He demands as due to His own dignity—as if God Himself was proud.
   - He is not in the least worried about His dignity.
   - He wants you to know Him; He wants to give you Himself.
   - If you really get in touch with Him you will be humble—delightedly humble.
   - You will have put aside the silly nonsense about your own dignity.
   - He wants us humble so that we can truly know him, without being preoccupied with ourselves.

4. Do not imagine that if you meet a really humble man he will be what most people call "humble" nowadays.
   - He will not be a greasy, smarmy person who is always telling you that he is a nobody.
   - He would probably strike you as someone who took a real interest in you and what you said to him.
   - If you disliked him at all it would probably be because you were envious of anyone who seemed to enjoy life so easily.
   - He would not be thinking about humility; he would not be thinking about himself at all.

If anyone wanted to acquire humility, Lewis volunteers the first step in the process. The first step is to realize that one is proud. Nothing whatever can be done before this.

Summary of Chapter 8

- Pride is a complete anti-God state of mind; it is thinking first and only of oneself.
- Pride leads to every other vice.
- Pride is competitive—it gets no pleasure out of having something, only out of having more of it than the next man.
- Lewis addresses four common misunderstandings about Pride.

Questions

1. Lewis thinks that on the issue of Pride is where Christian morals differ most sharply from all other moral systems. Do you agree or disagree? Don't quote, "Who am I to disagree with C. S. Lewis," to get out of this. Can you give some examples from other moral systems to back up your case?
2. Lewis seems to imply that serious Christians are probably more aware of Pride than others, and, as a consequence, are more concerned that they not offend in this way. Do you agree or disagree? Can you demonstrate with examples of "social" Christians (Patrick Morley's term) and those of other or no faith(s)?

3. Lewis writes, "as long as you are proud, you cannot know God." This is a very serious declaration. There is not a man of us who is not proud at times even in the worst sense. What are we to do? Is there any hope for any of us?

4. Lewis gives a two part test to determine if there is pride in our spiritual lives. Did you take the test as you read the chapter? Did you pass? What do you think of his test? Is this something you ought to remember and check yourself on periodically?

5. Lewis contrasts vanity with what he labels "real black, diabolical Pride." Can you differentiate between these concepts? Why do you suppose he gives Pride such a label?

6. Lewis addresses four common misunderstandings concerning Pride. Cite an example of each and determine whether your example involves Pride or pride.

7. Lewis thinks "control" is behind Pride. Do you agree or disagree? Cite some illustrations to back up your case.

9. Charity

Introduction

In a previous chapter, Lewis wrote that there are four "Cardinal" (key) virtues and three "Theological" virtues. The Cardinal virtues he identified for us as Prudence, Temperance, Justice, and Fortitude, and he described these virtues to us in that chapter. He left for another time identifying the Theological virtues. They are Faith, Hope, and Charity (Love). In this chapter he discusses Charity and then Hope and Faith in the next three chapters.

The understanding of the word Charity has changed over the years, he notes.

- In Lewis' time, Charity had come to mean giving to the poor. And he pointed out how it came to have that limited meaning. If a man had "charity," giving to the poor was one of the most obvious things he did, and so people came to talk as though that were the whole of charity.
- Originally, Charity meant "Love in the Christian sense." Love in the Christian sense does not mean an emotion; it is not a matter of the feelings, but of the will. It is that state of the will which we naturally have about ourselves, and must learn to have about other people.

Since Lewis addressed the giving to the poor aspect of charity in the chapter on Social Morality, he is now ready to discuss charity in the broader sense of the word.

Charity or Love

Lewis described in the chapter on Forgiveness our love for ourselves and he uses this to illustrate here how we are to love others.

- Our *love* for ourselves, he wrote, does not necessarily mean that we *like* ourselves. It means that we wish our own good.

- In the same way, Christian Charity or Love for our neighbors is a different thing from *liking* or *affection*.

Lewis asserts that we all regard others in one of two different ways:
- We "like" or are "fond" of some people.
- We don't like or are not fond of others.

This natural liking is neither a sin nor a virtue. But what we do about it is either sinful or virtuous!
- Natural liking or affection for people makes it easier to be "charitable" towards them. It is normally our duty to encourage our affections—to like people as much as we can—not because this liking is the virtue in charity but because it is a help to it.
- It is also necessary to be careful that our liking for someone makes us uncharitable or even unfair to someone else. And it is also possible that our liking conflicts with our charity towards the person we like.

Now the way to become charitable is not found in trying to manufacture feelings of affection for others. Some of us are just not very affectionate, so this won't work. Then what are we to do?

Lewis suggests that the rule in this regard is simple and applies to each of us universally: "Do not waste time bothering whether you love your neighbor; act as if you did."
- If we behave as if we love someone, we will eventually come to really love him.
- If we hurt someone we dislike, we will eventually dislike him even more. If you do him a favor, you will find yourself disliking him less.

There is one exception to this rule: If you do him a favor, not to please God and obey the law of Charity, but to show him what a splendid person you are and then wait for him to fall all over himself thanking you, you may be in for a long wait. People are not fooled by sham behavior.

Christian charity may sound like a forced thing to those who don't understand. Here is the difference between a Christian and a non-Christian in this regard:

- The "worldly" man has only affections or "likings." The worldly man treats certain people kindly because he likes them.
- The Christian man has only charity. He tries to treat everyone kindly, and finds himself liking more and more people in the bargain.

Unfortunately, this same law works powerfully in the opposite direction. The crueler you are, the more you will hate; and the more you hate, the crueler you will become.

As we have seen, Lewis is big on gains and losses as beachheads for future gains or retreats for future losses.

- The smallest good act today is the capture of a strategic point from which, a few months later, you may be able to go on to victories you never imagined.
- An apparently trivial indulgence in lust or anger today is the loss of a strategic position from which the enemy might gain a foothold.

Godward Charity

Sometimes people use the word charity not only to describe Christian love between humans, but also God's love for humans and man's love for God.

- God's love toward us is a much safer thing to think about than our love towards Him. It is not in doubt.
- But what if we feel that we don't have feelings of affection for God? Act as if you did. Ask yourself, "What would I do if I was sure I loved God?" Then do it.

Christian love, either towards others or towards God, is an act of the will. If we are obeying the commandment, "Love the Lord your God ..." He will give us feelings of love if He pleases.

Our feelings may come and go, but His love for us is constant. It is not wearied by our sins, or our indifference. Therefore it is relentless in its determination that we are cured of those sins, at whatever cost to us, at whatever cost to Him.

Summary of Chapter 8

- Charity means more than giving to the poor. It is love in the Christian sense
- Charity is loving others and loving God.
- Charity is an act of the will; it is something we do, not something we feel.

Questions

1. Do you understand the difference between what Lewis would call charity and Charity? Can you explain the difference and how it came to be?
2. Lewis writes that it is not a sin not to like, or even to dislike others. This is a difficult notion to accept. Do you understand this? What is a sin is not to love someone because you don't like them. Explain.
3. Do you agree that how you treat someone determines ultimately how you regard them? If you treat people with Christian love, you may indeed come to love them. What if, regardless of how kind you are to someone, they still aren't kind in return? What are you to do? Is it ever OK just to write someone off and avoid them?
4. Do you understand the difference between worldly and Christian love? Can you think of some specific examples to illustrate the concept?

5. Do you sometimes find it is difficult to have feelings of affection for God? Lewis gives a good prescription for this condition. What is it?
6. Do you occasionally feel that God's love for you depends on how "good" you are? Of course, we know that this is not true—He loves us unconditionally. Do you understand why it is so important to Him that you are addressing the areas of sin in your life (with His help)?

10. Hope

Hope Defined

The Theological virtues are Faith, Hope, and Charity (Love). Lewis discussed Charity in the previous chapter; in this chapter he discusses Hope and then Faith in the next two chapters.

Hope is a continual looking forward to the eternal world. It is not as some people think a form of escapism or wishful thinking.

Christians are meant to hope for the eternal world, but they are not to leave the present world as it is. An examination of history will confirm that the Christians who did the most for the present world were just those who thought most of the next:

- The Apostles themselves started the conversion of the Roman Empire from a pagan to a Christian culture.
- Many of the greatest artists and scientists were devout Christians—Newton, Faraday, and Paschal.
- The English Evangelicals who abolished the slave trade—William Wilberforce, John Newton, and others.

These men all left their mark on Earth because their minds were occupied with heaven. Lewis thought that in his own time it was because Christians had largely ceased to think of the other world that they had become ineffective in this. Aim at Heaven and you will get earth thrown in; aim at earth and you will get neither.

Lewis wrote that most of us find it very difficult to want Heaven at all—except insofar as Heaven means meeting again our friends who have died. He suggested two reasons for this:

- We have not been trained to hope. Our whole education process is geared to the present world. Our educational system teaches people how to earn a living, not how to live.
- We don't recognize hope when it is present. Most people when they do look into their own hearts know that they want, and want acutely, something that cannot be had in this world.

The longings that arise in us, that something we grasp at, just fades away in reality.

Hope Pursued

Lewis describes two wrong ways of pursuing hope, and one right way.

- The Fool's Way. The fool puts the blame on the things themselves.
  - He spends his whole life thinking that if he had just married another woman, or tried another profession, etc., he would have caught the mysterious something we are all after.
  - Most of the bored, discontented, rich people in the world are of this type. They go from woman to woman, continent to continent, always thinking that the latest is *the real thing*, and always disappointed.
- The Way of the Disillusioned Sensible Man. He decides that satisfaction is a fiction.
  - He says, "One feels that way when he is young, but when you reach my age, you've given up chasing the rainbow's end."
  - He settles down and learns not to expect too much and represses that part of himself, which, as he would say, used to "Ask for the moon."
  - He is apt to act rather superior towards what he calls, "adolescents," but gets along fairly comfortably.

This would be the best course if we could assume that men did not live forever. But suppose infinite happiness really is there, waiting for us? It would be a tragedy to find out too late (a moment after death) that we had deprived ourselves the opportunity of enjoying it.

- The Christian Way. The Christian says, "Creatures are not born with desires unless satisfaction for those desires exists."
  - If I find in myself a desire which no experience in this world can satisfy, the most probable explanation is that I was made for another world.

- If none of my earthly pleasures satisfies it, that does not prove that the universe is a fraud. Perhaps earthly pleasures were meant to arouse it.
  - I must never despise, or be unthankful for these earthly pleasures.
  - I must never mistake them for the something else of which they are only a copy.
- I must keep alive in myself the desire for my true country, which I shall not find until after death. I must make it the main object of life to press on to that other country and to help others do the same.

Finally, there is no need to be worried by facetious people who try to make the Christian hope of Heaven ridiculous by saying they don't want to spend eternity playing harps. They, of course misrepresent the imagery used in Scripture to describe the eternal world.

- Musical instruments are used to communicate ecstasy and infinity.
- Crowns suggest that those in heaven share God's splendor, power, and joy.
- Gold is mentioned to suggest the timeliness and preciousness of heaven.

The answer to such people is that if they can't understand books written for grown-ups, they should not talk about them.

Summary of Chapter 10

- Hope is looking forward to the eternal world.
- Christians are meant to hope for the eternal world, but they are not to leave the present world as it is.
- The Christian way is the only reasonable way of explaining and dealing with the longings of life.

Questions

1. Do you really look forward to the eternal world? Or do you have misgivings about dying and facing God? Perhaps you are like my friend who said he thought heaven would be a pretty boring place because all you did was sit around praising God all the time. Discuss.

2. Do you see that there is a tension between looking ahead for the eternal world and doing something about the present world? Most observers of history realize that Christianity has contributed powerfully for good in the world. Why do you suppose it is that Christians have had such a positive impact for good in the present world?

3. Do you agree that we have not been educated to hope—to look forward to the coming of God's Kingdom? Do you think Christian education institutions do a better job in this regard than secular ones? Why or why not? Do you see how we have painted ourselves into the corner so to speak by insisting that we limit our educational content to that which we can experience with our senses?

4. In 1 Corinthians 13:13, the Apostle Paul wrote, "But now faith, hope, love, abide these three; but the greatest of these is love." What does this mean? Does he mean that without love, it is not possible to have faith or hope? Or that if only one of the three virtues were possible, love would be preferred? Or something else entirely?

5. Do you know people who deal with longing the Fool's way? The Disillusioned Man's way? Which do you think is most prevalent in our culture? What might you say to an adherent of either philosophy in order to dissuade them from their position?

6. Do you see why it is important to understand that some of your deep longings may represent a desire for something that only heaven can fulfill? And do you see how these longings are actually a good thing in the sense that they remind us to make the main object of our lives to press on to that other country and to help other people to come along with us?

11. Faith

Faith as Belief

The Theological virtues are Faith, Hope, and Charity (Love). Lewis discussed Charity and Hope in previous chapters; he discusses Faith in this chapter and the next.

Christians mean two different things when they talk about Faith:
- In the first sense, Faith simply means belief—accepting or regarding as true the doctrines of Christianity.   And this is the topic he begins to address here.
- In the second sense, Faith means the realization that one is totally bankrupt and only God can help. Lewis talks about this sense of Faith later in this chapter and the next.

Lewis was puzzled that Christians regard Faith in the belief sense as a virtue; he couldn't understand what was moral or immoral about believing or not believing a set of statements. He thought that any sane individual accepted or rejected any statement, not because he wanted to or did not want to, but because the evidence seemed good or bad.
- If he were mistaken about the goodness or badness of the evidence, that would not mean that he was a bad man, but only that he was not very clever.
- If he thought the evidence bad, but tried to force himself to believe in spite of it, that would be merely stupid.

What Lewis confesses he did not see and that a good many people still do not see was as follows: if the human mind once accepts a thing as true, it will automatically go on regarding it as true, until some reason for reconsidering it turns up.

Lewis thought that the human mind was completely ruled by reason, but he came to see that there is always a battle going on in our minds.
- On one side is faith and reason.

- On the other side is emotion and imagination.

And he gives two examples to prove his point.
- Dealing with a pretty, but deceitful woman.
- Learning to swim as a young child.

The same processes are in play when Christianity is in question.
- If one's best reasoning tells him that the weight of evidence is against it, then the reasonable thing to do is to reject it.
- But suppose one's reason decides that the weight of evidence is for it. Lewis suggests that certain circumstances will arise, for example,
  - Some sort of bad news.
  - Trouble of some kind.
  - Influence of unbelievers.
  And all at once his emotions will rise up and carry out a sort of blitz against his belief.

Lewis is not talking here of moments at which any real reasons against Christianity turn up—these always must be faced, and this is a different matter. Here he is talking about moments when a mere mood rises up against belief.

Faith in the belief sense of the word is the art of holding on to things your reason has once accepted, in spite of your changing moods.
- When Lewis was an atheist, he says, there were times in which Christianity looked terribly probable.
- Having become a Christian, he confesses there are times in which the whole thing looks very improbable.

This rebellion of your moods against your real self is going to happen. This is why Faith is such a necessary virtue; unless you teach your emotions "where they get off," you can never be either a sound Christian or even a sound atheist. One must train the habit of Faith. He suggested two ways of doing this:

- The first step is to recognize the fact that our moods or emotions change. There is nothing to be alarmed about when this happens—it is a fact of life.
- The second step is to make sure that once you have accepted Christianity, then some of its main doctrines will be deliberately considered every day.

We have to be continually reminded of what we believe. Neither this belief nor any other will automatically remain alive in the mind. It must be fed. Think about people who have turned away from Christianity; in most cases, they drift slowly away.

Faith as Acceptance

Lewis now turns to Faith in the second or "higher" sense of the word. In the rest of the chapter, he just lays the groundwork for the discussion he will attempt in the next chapter. He suggests that this is the most difficult thing he has attempted to explain so far.

He wants us to return to consider what he said about Humility.
- The first step towards humility was to realize that one is proud.
- The second step is to make a serious attempt to practice humility.

A week is not long enough for this, he says. Things will go OK for a week. We should try to practice humility for six weeks. In the process of practicing humility (or any other Christian virtue) for an extended period, Lewis thinks we will discover two important truths about ourselves:
- No one knows how bad he is until he has tried very hard to be good
  - This is why bad people, in one sense, know very little about badness. We never discover the strength of the evil impulse inside us until we try to fight it.
  - Jesus, because He was the only man who never yielded to temptation, is the only man who knows to the full what temptation means.

- The main thing we learn from a serious attempt to practice the Christian virtues (humility or any other) is that we fail.
  - Any idea that we could perform our side of the contract and thus put God in our debt so that in fairness He had to perform His side must be forgotten.
  - Lewis thought that most people before becoming Christians think of it as a kind of exam or bargain. This notion must be destroyed.
  - God has been waiting for the moment when we discover that there is no question of earning a passing mark on His exam, or putting Him in our debt.
- If we devoted every moment of our whole life to serving Him, we could not give Him anything that He did not already own.

Once we have discovered these two truths, God can really begin to work in our lives. It is after this that life really begins. We can now go on to talk of Faith in the second sense.

Summary of Chapter 11

Christians think of Faith in two different ways:
- The first way is simply in the sense of belief—specifically in the Christian doctrines.
- In order to understand the second sense of Faith one must discover two truths.
  - We can't make it on our own.
  - We can't do anything for God.

It is only when we understand these prerequisites, that we can really live the Christian life.

Questions

1. Do you understand that there is a conflict between reason and faith on the one hand and emotions and imagination in your mind? Can you relate a recent experience in which you were

aware of the conflict? Can you identify some of the things that are likely to set off your imagination or emotions?

2. Lewis confesses that as a mature Christian he sometimes has doubts about the whole Christian scene. Have you ever experienced doubts about your Christian faith? If you have, do you see that this is a normal thing—nothing of which to be ashamed or embarrassed?

3. Lewis gives an effective antidote for doubts—holding the Christian doctrines before our consideration on a regular basis. The Apostle Paul had a similar antidote—"So faith comes from hearing, and hearing by the word of Christ (Romans 10:17)." Do you see that this is why we periodically recite the various Christian creeds in worship? Are you reminding yourself regularly of what you believe?

4. Have you ever seriously attempted to practice some Christian virtue for an extended period of time? Did you succeed? Of course not! Is this a good thing or a bad thing? If you learned that you cannot be good on your own, you learned a valuable lesson.

5. Did you ever think of Christianity as a test? God is the examiner and you are the examinee? Remember, God doesn't grade on the curve. His standard is 100% or you fail. Do you see why this approach to living the Christian life doesn't work?

6. Does God need anything you have? Do you see that you could serve Him 24/7 and you would still be in His debt? Do you understand that you cannot work hard enough or long enough to put yourself in God's debt?

12. Faith

Faith as Surrender

In the last chapter, Lewis informed us that Faith can be considered in two different senses:

- In the first sense, Faith simply means belief—accepting or regarding as true the doctrines of Christianity. Lewis discussed Faith in the sense of belief as the primary focus of Chapter 11.
- In the second sense, Faith means the realization that one is totally bankrupt and only God can help. Lewis also laid the foundation for his discussion of Faith in the sense of bankruptcy in Chapter 11.

In this chapter he will finish his discussion of what he calls the higher sense of Faith. Before he begins, he wants to warn the reader that he or she might not be ready for this material; if so, it should be dropped at once. Lewis gives several reasons for this:

- There are certain things in Christianity that can be understood from the outside, before one has become a Christian.
- There are a great many things that cannot be understood until after you have come a distance along the Christian road.

And Faith in the higher sense, he claims, is one of these. Lewis suggests that whenever we come to something in Christianity that we don't understand, we should let it alone. Most probably, we will discover its meaning in the future.

Now, here is what he had covered as foundational in the previous chapter:

- It is only after a man has tried his level best to practice the Christian virtues, and found that he fails, that he realizes his own bankruptcy.
- Moreover, even if one could perfectly observe the Christian virtues, he would only be giving God what He is justly due.

God is not so much interested in our actions as He is our character—He desires for us to become the kind of creatures He intended us to be—creatures related to Him in a certain way. And if we are related to Him as we ought to be, we will inevitably be right with all of our fellow creatures.

Lewis underscores that until we understand who God is and who we are we cannot experience Faith in the higher sense. He identifies two wrong concepts of God that prevent us from getting it:
- Thinking of God as an examiner who has given us a sort of paper or exercise to complete.
- Thinking of God as the opposite party in some sort of bargaining deal with claims and counter claims.

Two aspects of trying are important here:
- Unless we really try hard before failing, there will always be at the back of our minds the idea that if we try harder next time we will succeed in being completely good.
- In the final analysis, it is not trying that carries the day for us—it is when we turn to God and say, "You must do this, I can't."

Lewis warns that we don't need to be too introspective here for several reasons.
- When we start asking ourselves *if* we have come to this point, or *when* we came to this point, we have missed the idea.
- We may not come to the point in a sudden flash—it may happen to us gradually over an extended period of time.

It is the change from being confident about our own efforts to the state in which we despair of doing anything for ourselves and leave it to God; this is what is important. Not when it happened or how.

When we finally come to this realization, that we are bankrupt and that only God can do it for us, two important things happen.

- Christ will somehow share with us the perfect human obedience which He carried out from His birth to His crucifixion.
- Christ will make us more like Himself, in a sense, He will make good our deficiencies—He will share His "sonship" with us.

In other words, He offers something for nothing: He offers everything for nothing. The whole Christian life consists in accepting this very remarkable offer. The difficulty is realizing that all we have done and can do is nothing.

What we would have liked is for God to count our good points and ignore our bad ones. It doesn't work this way.

Faith and Works

Handing everything over to Christ does not mean that we stop trying. To trust Him means, of course, trying to do all that He commands us to do. But it means trying in a new way:
- Not doing these things in order to be saved, but because He has saved us already.
- Not hoping to get to heaven as a reward for good actions, but because of the faint gleam of heaven in us.

Some Christians have asked which is most important Faith or Works. It seems as though there are two parodies (faulty versions) of the truth here.
- Some have said, "Good actions are all that matters." But the truth is that good actions done for the wrong motive are not good actions at all. Heaven cannot be bought—with money or anything else.
- Others have said, "Faith is all that matters." But if what we call faith in Christ does not involve taking the slightest notice of what He commands us to do, then it is not faith at all, but intellectual acceptance of some theory about Him.

In a rare moment, Lewis quotes the Scripture to resolve the dilemma, "Work out your salvation with fear and trembling; for it is God who is at work in you, both to will and to work for His good pleasure (Philippians 2:12-13).

- The first part of this verse looks like we do everything and God does nothing.
- The second part looks like God does everything and we do nothing.

And Lewis observes that this is just the sort of thing we come up against in Christianity—in trying to force God into little water-tight compartments. But God is not like this. He is at once inside us and outside us. We can't say who is doing what.

So Christianity seems at first to be all about morality, all about duties and rules and guilt and virtue. But then it leads on to something beyond, where we are filled with goodness, but we are not thinking about the goodness, we are too busy looking at the source.

Summary of Chapter 12

Faith in the higher sense is realizing that we are totally bankrupt and that only God can live the Christian life for us. When we finally come to this realization, that we are bankrupt and that only God can do it for us, two important things happen.

- Christ will somehow share with us the perfect human obedience which He carried out from His birth to His crucifixion.
- Christ will make us more like Himself, in a sense, He will make good our deficiencies—He will share His "sonship" with us.

Questions

1. Have you ever tried very hard over an extended period of time to live Christianly? What happened? Did you succeed? Do

you realize that in your own effort you can never succeed in this regard? As Romans 3:12 puts it, "All have turned away, they have together become worthless; there is no one who does good, not even one."

2. When you finally realize that you can't succeed in living the Christian life, rather than being a real downer, this is a wonderful turning point. Why? What is the alternative if you can't successfully live in such a way to merit God's approval?

3. What is your mental construct of God? Do you view Him as One who has given you a test to complete and is just waiting for you to fail so He can hammer you? Or do you see Him as One with whom you negotiate, "If You will do so and so, I will do such and such." Or do you view Him as One who will live the life He desires of you for you?

4. Do you understand why Lewis calls this the higher sense of Faith? Many people believe in the foundational doctrines of the Christian Faith (Faith in the ordinary sense). And many of them are gutting it out trying to follow Christ's commands in their own strength. Few have come to the point where they throw in the towel and say, "Lord, You do this, I can't."

5. Do you see that asking which is most important Faith or Works is the wrong question? We should ask what the role of Faith and Works is in the Christian life. Ephesians 2:8-10 is also a good reference for this point.

6. Having read and understood Ephesians 2:8-10 do you now see how Faith and Works are related in the Christian life? Can you explain it to someone? What would you say to James, the brother of Jesus, who wrote, "Faith without works is dead (James 2:26)?"

Book 4. Beyond Personality: Or First Steps In The Doctrine Of The Trinity

1. Making and Begetting

Theology

Theology is the study of God. As Lewis begins to explore the doctrine of the Trinity, he understands that he is launching out into theological waters. He allows as how people have warned him not to get into theology, but he goes ahead anyway for two reasons:

- First, anyone who wants to think about God at all should have the clearest, most accurate picture of Him that is available.
- Second, he doesn't want to treat his readers as children, sparing them the difficult aspects of the Christian faith.

Lewis recalls a conversation with an R.A.F. officer which convinced him that theology is essential. This gentleman held that there were two views of God:

- The Experiential View. The officer claimed to have experienced the mystery of God out in the desert. To him this was the real God.
- The Theoretical View. The officer suggested that Lewis' view of God consisted of neat little dogmas and formulas about God.

Lewis uses the idea of a map to suggest that the officer's perception, while sounding good, was indeed faulty. When we choose to represent some geographical features with a map several things must be taken into consideration.

- First, there is the real terrain we are choosing to represent. It may be a city, part of the countryside, a coastline, an ocean. Whatever it is we happen to be considering, it is a real entity. It exists in reality.
- Second, we have experiences with whatever fragment of the terrain we are considering. We have visited the city; we have been to the seashore. But our experience is not the reality of the

geographical feature.

Lewis is willing to grant that the map is for sure just colored paper, but the map has some very important advantages for helping us understand the reality in question.

- For one thing, the map embeds the combined experience (and expertise) of many people who participated in its construction. It is almost as though we combined all of the different experiences people have had with the reality into one composite.
- For another thing, if we want to go to someplace other than where we presently are, the map is absolutely essential. It won't do any good to imagine we are in New York, or at the beach, we must follow the map to experience the reality of interest.

Lewis goes on to suggest that the map is like theology. Christian doctrines are not the end to which we desire to go.

- Doctrines are not God. They are only a map, but they are based on the combined experiences of many people who have really been in touch with God and who have systematically articulated what He is like.
- If we want to go beyond our limited experiences with God, which are no doubt real, we have to go beyond the experiences to the doctrines which describe the reality that is God.

So Lewis has no use for vague religions based on feelings about finding God in nature or whatever. He says you will not get eternal life by "feeling the presence of God in flowers or music."

Lewis thinks theology to be practical. In earlier times, one might have been able to get by on a few simple ideas about God, but in modern times when many conflicting ideas are floating around and much debate is taking place theology is necessary. Otherwise, we are on dangerous ground.

- We may have a lot of wrong ideas about God—ideas that are out-of-date, which real Theologians tried centuries ago and rejected.
- Or we may buy into some of the popular new ideas that are simply not true—such as the idea that Jesus was a great moral teacher, if we just follow His advice we will have peace and avoid war.

Lewis suggests that, while true, this last insight is not practical at all. We have never followed the advice of great moral teachers, why is Jesus any different? We are probably less likely to follow His advice because His ideas go far beyond those of other moral teachers. If Christianity is only another bit of moral advice, it is of no importance.

Sons of God

But Christianity is more than moral advice. Its claims go far beyond that.
- Christianity affirms that Jesus is the Son of God.
- Christianity affirms that those who put their trust in Jesus can become Sons of God also.
- Christianity affirms that the death of Jesus saves us from our sins.
- Christianity claims to be telling us about another world, behind the one we experience.

Are these teachings difficult? Yes. Does that imply that they are false, just because they are hard? Not at all.

Lewis thinks the one Christian teaching that causes the most difficulty is the statement that by attaching ourselves to Christ, we can become Sons of God. People reply, "Aren't we Sons of God already?" To which Lewis replies, "Only in the sense that God has brought us into existence and looks after us is He like a father." But the Bible is talking about something entirely different. And this is where we must turn to theology.

So we must examine the Christian creed that says that Christ is the Son of God, "begotten, not created." What does this mean?

- This has nothing to do with the fact that Jesus was born on earth as a man.
- It has nothing to do with His being born of a virgin—the Virgin Birth.

We are thinking about something that happened before the universe was created, before time began. We need to look at the phrase, "Before all the worlds, Christ is begotten, not created."

- To beget is to become the father of. When you beget, you beget something of the same kind as yourself. A man begets humans; a beaver begets beavers.
- To create is to make something. When you create, you make something of a different kind than yourself. A man might create a computer; a beaver creates dams and lodges.

What God begets is God, just as man begets man. What God creates is not God, just as what man creates is not man. This is why men are not Sons of God in the same sense that Christ is. Men may be like God in certain ways, but they are not things of the same kind.

Lewis describes how everything God has made (created) has some likeness to Himself.

- Space is like Him in its vastness.
- Matter is like Him in that it has energy.
- The plant world is like Him in the sense that it is alive. But this life is not the same as that which is in God, it is not eternal, it is not self-existent.
- The animal kingdom is like Him in the sense that it multiplies itself. A resemblance to the unceasing activity and creativity of God.
- In the higher mammals we have the beginnings of instinctive affection, not the love which is in God, but like it.
- In man we get the most complete resemblance to God. Man lives, loves and reasons. But this is Biological life, not Spiritual life.

And here is how Lewis differentiates between the two.

- Biological life (Bios) comes to us through nature. It is always tending to run down and decay. It can only be sustained by inputs from nature (the environment) in the form of air, water, food.
- Spiritual life (Zoe) which is in God from all eternity, and which made the whole natural universe. It is eternal and it is self-existent.

A man who changed from having Bios to having Zoe would have gone through as big a change as a statue which changed from being a carved stone to being a real man. This is Christianity. The world is a great sculptor's shop. There is a rumor going around the shop that some of us some day are going to come to life.

Summary of Chapter 1

Lewis makes an important distinction between knowing God experientially and knowing God from understanding doctrines about Him. We must understand the important Christian doctrines, lest we allow our experiences distort or restrict our view of God.

Christianity is not just some more moral advice from another moral teacher. It makes some revolutionary claims, among which are:
- Christianity affirms that Jesus is the Son of God.
- Christianity affirms that those who put their trust in Jesus can become Sons of God also.

In order to understand what it means to become a Son of God, we must understand the difference between begetting and creating and the difference between Biological life (Bios) and Spiritual life (Zoe).
- Biological life comes to us through nature.
- Spiritual life is the eternal, self-existent life of God.

Created living things possess Biological life. When we put our trust in Jesus, God imparts to us Spiritual life, and we become His Sons.

Questions

1. Do you understand the distinction between the two views of God Lewis describes—I call them the Experiential and the Theoretical view? Do you know people whose lives are impacted by their experiential view of God? Can you see how one's view of God experientially could distort or restrict their understanding of God?
2. Lewis uses the map as an illustration to show us why theology is so very important. Was this a helpful device for you? Do you think sometimes we tend to avoid theology because we think it is difficult or too hard for us? Should we?
3. Can you think of any examples of out-of-date ideas that are currently being embraced by people even though theologians have debunked the same ideas centuries ago? Hint: there are quite a few. In fact some of them are floating around in the culture this very minute, keeping people from knowing the real God.
4. Have you ever heard someone say that Jesus was a great moral teacher and if we would just follow His commands, we would have peace and all live happily ever after? How would you respond now to such a statement? Remember, we don't want to turn people off—we want them to think through the faults in such logic.
5. Do you understand the distinction between begetting and creating? Do you understand the difference between Biological life and Spiritual life? Do you see why these concepts are fundamental to Christianity? The most important fact one can know is whether he or she has eternal life. Spiritual or biological life? How do we get it?
6. What would you say to someone whom you knew who was obviously not a believer who said, "Oh, we are all Sons of God. After all He created all men, didn't He?"

2. The Three-Personal God

A Personal God

In the last chapter Lewis explained the difference between making and begetting, and he suggested that what God begets is God, something of the same kind as Himself. Now he wants to push this notion a bit to consider a personal God.

Some people say, "I believe in a God, but not in a personal God." What they really mean to say is:
- There is a mysterious something which is beyond all other things, but it must be more than a person.
- They think that God is beyond personality, they really think of Him as something impersonal.

Lewis maintains that Christians are the only people who offer any idea of what a being that is beyond personality could be like. If you are looking for something super-personal, something more than a person, it is not a question of choosing between the Christian idea and other ideas. The Christian idea is the only game in town.

Some people believe that after this life, or perhaps after several lives [those who believe in reincarnation], human souls will be absorbed into God. But this view has problems.
- They mean that it is like one material thing being absorbed into another like a drop of water slipping into the sea.
- If this is what happens to us after our life is [lives are] over, then being absorbed is the same as ceasing to exist.

How can human souls be taken into the life of God and yet remain themselves? This is the sixty-four dollar question. Lewis suggests that only Christianity can answer this.
- When this happens, we become very much more ourselves than we were before, that is, when we were alive.

- And when we are thus taken into the life of God, the whole purpose for which we exist is accomplished.

Lewis uses the three Dimensions to illustrate the notion of being taken into God's life.
- If we are limited to only one dimension, the only figures we can sketch on a piece of paper are dots and lines.
- By adding a second dimension, we may draw figures, for example a square, which is composed of four lines.
- If we have three dimensions, we can construct what we call solid geometric shapes, for example a cube made up of six squares.

Now Lewis extends this illustration into the spiritual (or theological) world.
- He likens the human level to the two-dimensional world. Everything is simple. One person is one being, and any two persons are two separate beings. Just as a square is one figure and any two squares are two separate figures.
- On the divine level we still have personalities, but they are combined in new ways which we, who do not live on that level, cannot imagine. In God's dimension, we find a Being who is three Persons while remaining one Being. Just as a cube is six squares combined into a cube.

Lewis admits several things about where we have now landed.
- We can never fully conceive of a Being like this, just as if we lived in a two-dimensional world, we couldn't conceive of three-dimensional figures.
- But even so, we are now just beginning to get a faint notion of something super-personal—something more than a person.
- And it is something we could never have guessed, and yet, it fits in with all the things we know already.

One might ask, "If we cannot imagine a three-personal Being, what is the good of talking about Him?" And Lewis suggests that the important thing is being actually drawn into the three-personal life.

To illustrate this he imagines a Christian kneeling down to say his prayers, trying to get in touch with God. The man knows several things about this transaction:

- That it is really God who is prompting him to pray in the first place—God, so to speak, inside him.
- That all of his real knowledge of God comes through Christ, the Man who is God—Christ is standing beside him helping him to pray.
- God is the thing to whom he is praying—the goal he is trying to reach. God is also the road or bridge along which he is being pushed to the goal.

The man is being caught up into the higher kind of life—what Lewis called Zoe or spiritual life; he is being pulled into God, by God, while remaining himself.

Knowing God

Before Jesus, people knew about God in a vague way. Then along came Jesus, a man who claimed to be God:

- He was not the sort of man you could dismiss as a lunatic. He made them believe Him.
- They met Him again after they had seen Him killed—they were witnesses of His resurrection.
- After that, when they had been formed into a little society or community, they found God somehow inside them, directing them.
- And when they worked it all out, they found that they had arrived at the Christian definition of the three-personal God.

When it comes to knowing God, the initiative lies with Him.

- If He does not reveal Himself to you, nothing you can possibly do will enable you to find Him.
- It is impossible for Him to show Himself to a man whose whole mind and character are in the wrong condition.

- He shows more of Himself to some than to others, not because He has favorites, but because their hearts are right.

Lewis suggests that the instrument through which we see God is our whole self. If our self is not kept clean and bright, our glimpse of God will be blurred. He concludes from this a couple of principles:
- Some nations have horrible religions, because they have been looking at God through a distorted lens.
- God shows Himself as He really is not simply to men who are individually good, but to men who are united together in a body, loving one another, helping one another, showing Him to one another.

Thus, the one really adequate instrument for learning about God is the whole Christian community, waiting for Him together. Christian brotherhood [fellowship] is necessary for knowing God.

If Christianity were something we had made up, it could have been made a lot easier. We are dealing with facts. Anyone can be simple if he has no facts to bother about.

Summary of Chapter 2

To illustrate what it means to be taken into God's life. Lewis uses the example of a man on his knees praying to God. The man knows several things about this transaction:
- That it is really God who is prompting him to pray in the first place—God, so to speak, inside him.
- That all of his real knowledge of God comes through Christ, the Man who is God—Christ is standing beside him helping him to pray.
- God is the thing to whom he is praying—the goal he is trying to reach. God is also the road or bridge along which he is being pushed to the goal.

It is only because God has allowed Himself to be known by us that we can even begin to understand how He can be at once the force behind the universe and One who loves and cares for us individually.

Questions

1. Do you agree that many people have difficulty seeing God in a personal way? Remember the **Star Wars** movies? God was referred to in an off-hand way as *The Force.* Do you see how such an understanding of God could prevent someone from ever knowing Him as Jesus described it in the gospels?

2. Do you see the problem encountered in some of the Eastern religions that suggest that when we come to the end of our life (lives) we simply are united with the Power? What is wrong with this view? Would you trade the assurance you have in Christ for eternal life as a unique person for what they are offering?

3. Lewis says that "when we are taken into the life of God, we become very much more ourselves than we were before." What does this mean? He also says that "being taken into the life of God is the very purpose for which we exist." What does this mean? Is this an important concept?

4. The illustration of how God is involved with the believer who is seeking Him through prayer is, as the Brits say, spot on when it comes to showing what it means to be taken into God's life. Do you understand all that is happening here? Do you understand how you are every bit as much an individual as anyone else when God is involved with you in these ways—as He always is?

5. Do you agree with Lewis that nations (people) who look at God through a distorted lens may indeed have a distorted religion? How does this apply to Islam? How does it apply to Eastern religions? How does it apply to Judaism, or does it?

6. In this chapter Lewis makes a strong case for believers belonging to the body of Christ which is the church. Do you know people who say they can commune with God just as well in nature or in their living room as in church? What would you say to them having read this material?

3. Time and Beyond Time

God and Time

Lewis suggests that in the present chapter he will touch on a topic that may be helpful to some readers and an unnecessary complication for others. If you are one who isn't much concerned with how the notion of time is reconciled with God who is beyond time, he would have you proceed to the next chapter without bothering with this one. He offers two reasons for suggesting this:

- He thinks it is "silly" when reading a book that there seems to be an unwritten rule that the reader must not skip.
- Sensible people should skip over material which they suspect is going to be of no use to them whatever.

Here is how Lewis puts the issue of God and time before us. Someone put it to him by saying, "I can believe in God all right, but what I can't swallow is the idea of Him attending to several hundred million human beings that are all addressing Him at the same moment." And Lewis thought that a lot of people were troubled by this.

He rightly points out that the trouble comes in the words *at the same moment*. And he continues to go to the root of the issue—the idea of God having to fit too many things into one moment of time. To explain this he considers how time constrains us as humans and then he looks at the issue of time from God's perspective.

First from a human perspective:

- Our lives come to us moment by moment. One moment disappears before the next comes along; and there is room for very little in each.
- So we take it for granted that this Time series—this arrangement of past, present, and future—is the way all things really exist.
- We assume that the whole universe, including God Himself, is always moving on from past to future just as we do.

119

But many learned men do not believe this. Theologians first discovered that some things are not in time; then philosophers, and finally scientists.

From God's perspective, time is altogether different from ours.
- God is almost certainly not in time. His life does not consist of moments following one another.
- Every moment from the beginning of time is always the Present for Him; God has no past and He has no future.

Lewis uses the idea of an author writing a novel to illustrate how God is not subject to time in the same ways that we are.
- As an author, one can write about a character caught up in some intense drama, and at the very moment of crisis, he can save his file and close his computer.
- The author can think about the character in a time dimension external to the one in the story, or he could do other things as well, with no impact on the story.

Now this illustration has several important implications for our understanding of how time impacts God.
- God is not hurried along in the Time-stream of this universe any more than the author of a novel is hurried by the imaginary time of his story.
- God has infinite attention to spare for each individual. He does not have to deal with us en masse.
- You are as much alone with Him as if you were the only being He had ever created. When Jesus died, He died for you individually as though you were alone in the world.

Lewis admits that there are limitations to his illustration.
- The author of a novel moves from the imaginary time dimension to the real time dimension when he puts the novel aside.
- God does not live in any time series at all. His life is not dribbled out moment by moment as ours is.

- God's life is Himself. If we picture time as a straight line along which we must travel, then God is the whole page upon which the line is drawn.

We come to the parts of the line one by one; God contains the whole line and sees it all.

Resolving Difficulties

Lewis thinks it is worth trying to grasp these ideas because they clear up at least two difficulties that the notion of associating time with God presents us.

The first difficulty is as follows: Christians believe that the eternal God who is everywhere and keeps the whole universe going, once became a human being. Here is the rub.

- How did the universe continue to run during the time when God was a baby, or while He was asleep?
- How could God at the same time be God who knows everything and also a man who asked His disciples, "Who touched Me?"

In other words, we assume that Christ's life as God was in time, and that His life as the man Jesus in Palestine was a shorter period taken out of that time. But we cannot fit Christ's earthly life in Palestine into any time-relations with His life as God beyond all space and time for these reasons:

- God has no history and He has no future. He is too completely and utterly real to have either.
- To have a history means losing part of your reality (because some of it has slipped away into the past).
- To have a future means not being in possession of all of your reality (because some of it is still in the future).

[When Jesus told the Pharisees, "Before Abraham was born, I AM," He was affirming this aspect of God's nature. John 8:58]

A second difficulty we get if we believe that God is in time is: Everyone who believes in God at all believes that He knows what you and I are going to do tomorrow."

- If He knows I am going to do so-and-so, how can I be free to do otherwise? In other words, how can I truly have free-will?
- The problem comes from thinking that God is progressing along a time line like we do—He can see ahead, but we cannot.
- If it is true that God foresees our acts, it would be very hard to understand how we could be free not to do them.

But if God is outside of and above the time dimension, what we call "tomorrow" is visible to Him in the same way as what we call "today." All the days are "Now" for Him.

- So He does not foresee you doing things tomorrow; He simply sees you doing them, because though tomorrow is not yet there for you, it is for Him.
- You never think that your actions at this moment are any less free because God knows that you are doing them.
- He knows your tomorrow's actions in just the same way— because He is already in tomorrow and can simply watch you.

Thus the fact that God is omniscient about our actions really has nothing to do with whether or not we are free to act in whatever way we choose in regard to moral choices.

Summary of Chapter 3

Christians sometimes have trouble understanding God because they want to put Him in the same time constrained life that we live. The truth in this regard is:

- Our lives come to us moment by moment. One moment disappears before the next comes along; and there is room for very little in each.
- Every moment from the beginning of time is always the Present for God; He has no past and He has no future.

Understanding that God is not constrained by time helps us to resolve two troubling difficulties of the Christian faith.

- How did the universe continue to run during the time when God was a baby, or while He was asleep?
- If He knows I am going to do so-and-so, how can I be free to do otherwise? In other words, how can I truly have free-will?

Questions

1. Have you ever struggled with some of the issues Lewis covers in this chapter—how could God be both God and a human named Jesus *at the same time* or how can we be free if God knows ahead of time what we are going to do? Was this material helpful or did you decide to punt it?

2. Do you agree that we live our lives one moment at a time and that the present moment disappears before the next comes along? Do you see how we constrain God when we insist that He lives in the same type of time-dimensioned reality that we inhabit? Explain.

3. Do you see that if every moment from the beginning of time and every future moment is always present before God, then He truly operates in a very different way than we must? Do you see as Lewis suggests that this freedom from the press of time allows Him to devote individual attention to every believer at once as if that person was the only person in the universe? Does this make you feel special?

4. Do you understand the notion that God has no past and He has no future? As Jesus said, "Before Abraham was born, I AM." God is completely self-existent—He exists apart from anything else and independent of anything else, including time. Thus when we try to fit Him into our concepts of time, we don't understand Him as He really is. Do you see this?

5. Does understanding this aspect of the nature of God enable you to see how He can at the same time be the God of the universe and the Savior of the world? Do you think you could explain this idea to a friend who was struggling with this very problem in trying to understand Christianity?

6. Do you see that even though God knows what moral choices we will make at every moment of our lives, we are still perfectly free to make whatever choices we desire to make? Could you explain this idea to a friend who was struggling with the notion of free will in trying to understand Christianity?

4. Good Infection

Three Persons

In this chapter, Lewis further describes the nature of the triune God, a Being who consists of three Persons while remaining one Being. He begins the discussion by giving an example to show that each Person of the Trinity has always existed—one did not come before the others.

Consider two books, A and B, lying on a table, one book on top of the other. Suppose that the books have always been in that position on the table.

- If A is the book on the bottom, we say that the position of A is causing the position of B. So B is not touching the table, but is an inch or so above the table.
- B's position would always have been a result of A's position. But because they had both always been there, A's position did not exist before B's.

In other words, the result (B's position) did not come after the cause (A's position). Normally the result comes after the cause, but not always. And Lewis thinks it important to consider the exceptional case.

In trying to explain how three Persons are connected, we have to use words which make it sound as if one of them was there before the others. But this is not so.

- The First Person [of the Trinity] is called the Father. We say that the Father begets the Second; we call it begetting because what is begotten is of the same kind as the Father.
- The Second Person is the Son. The Son exists because the Father exists; but there was never a time before the Father begot the Son. There is no before and after about it at all.
- We must think always of the Son as streaming forth from the Father, like light from a lamp, or heat from a fire, or thoughts from a mind.

- The Son is the self-expression of the Father—what the Father has to say. And there never was a time when He wasn't saying it.
- The relationship between the Father and the Son is a relationship of love. The Father delights in His Son; the Son looks up to His Father.

Now before describing the Holy Spirit, Lewis returns to the notion that God is indeed not a single Person. He reminds us that people are fond of saying that "God is love."
- The statement, "God is love," has no real meaning unless God is at least two Persons. Love is something that one person has for another. If God were a single person, then before the world [and humans] was created, He was not love.
- What people really mean when they say "God is love" is something quite different. They mean "Love is God." They mean our feelings of love, however and wherever they arise, and whatever results they produce are special.
- What Christians mean by the statement "God is love" is that the living, dynamic activity of love has been going on in God forever, and this love has created everything else.

Lewis thinks this is the most important difference between Christianity and all other religions, that is, that in Christianity God is not a static thing—not even a person—but a dynamic, pulsating activity, a life, almost a kind of drama.

Now Lewis addresses the Holy Spirit. Continuing with the images he has been using, he says:
- The union between the Father and the Son is such a live, concrete thing that this union itself is also a Person.
- What grows out of the joint life of the Father and the Son is a real Person, the Third of the three Persons who are God.

Lewis warns us not to be worried or surprised if we find the Holy Spirit more vague or more ethereal than the Father or the Son. He thinks there is good reason for this: in the Christian life we are not usually looking at the Holy Spirit.

And Lewis gives us a word picture to help us understand the three Persons and their roles in our Christian life.
- The Father is that Someone "out there" in front of you.
- The Son is Someone standing at your side, helping you to pray, and trying to turn you into another son.
- The Holy Spirit is the Someone inside you, or behind you.

Considering the Holy Spirit from a different perspective, God is love, and that love works through men—especially through the Christian community. But this spirit of love is, from all eternity, a love going on between the Father and the Son.

So What?

Lewis thinks that understanding this is the most important thing in the world. The whole dance or drama or pattern of this three-Personal life is to be played out in each one of us. Each of us has to enter into that dance, that drama.

This is the only way for us to experience the happiness for which we were made. If you want joy, power, peace, eternal life, you must get close to, even into, the thing that has them.
- They are not a sort of prize which God could, if He chose, just hand out to anyone. They are a great fountain of energy and beauty spurting up at the center of reality.
- How could a man united to God not live forever? What can a man separated from God do but wither and die?

But how are we to be united to God? How is it possible to be taken into the three-Personal life? This is the whole offer which Christianity makes: we can, if we let God have His way, come to share in the life of Christ.
- We shall then be sharing in a life which was begotten, not made, which has always existed and always will exist.

- We shall also be sons of God. We shall love the Father as Christ does and the Holy Spirit will reside in us and empower us.

This is what Lewis means by "good infection." The whole purpose of becoming a Christian is to become like Christ.

Summary of Chapter 4

We have trouble describing the three Persons of God because the words we must use make it sound like one of them came before the others. This is simply not so.
- The First Person [of the Trinity] is called the Father. We say that the Father begets the Second; we call it begetting because what is begotten is of the same kind as the Father.
- The Second Person is the Son. The Son exists because the Father exists; but there was never a time before the Father begot the Son. There is no before and after about it at all.
- The union between the Father and the Son is such a live, concrete thing that this union itself is also a Person, the Holy Spirit.

The only way for us to experience the happiness for which we were made—joy, power, peace, eternal life—is to get close to, even into, the thing that has them.

This is the whole offer which Christianity makes: we can, if we let God have His way, come to share in the life of Christ.

Questions

1. Do you understand why it is so important that we know that the three Persons of the triune God have always existed? To think otherwise is to place one above the others, isn't it? What would you say to someone who insisted that the Father created the Son?

2. Lewis says "the Son is the self-expression of the Father—what the Father has to say." Does this remind you at all of John 1:1? Does this help you better understand the relationship between the Father and the Son?
3. Lewis thinks that when people say "God is love" they really mean "Love is God." Do you see that this is absolutely different from what Christians mean when they say that the love of God has been going on forever and it is what has created everything else?
4. Lewis suggests that the Holy Spirit is actually the union of the Father and the Son, and that this union is itself a living Being. Is this a helpful construct? If you were going to try to explain the Holy Spirit to an unbeliever, what would you say?
5. It is certain that most of us concentrate less on the Person of the Holy Spirit than the Father or the Son. Lewis himself even calls the Spirit "it" which is a pronoun used to reference a thing instead of a person. Do you agree with the reason Lewis thinks this is so? Why or why not?
6. "The whole offer which Christianity makes is that we can, if we let God have His way, come to share in the life of Christ." Do you understand this statement? Could you explain it to someone who was searching for meaning and purpose in life?

5. The Obstinate Toy Soldiers

Two Kinds of Life

The Son of God became a man to enable men to become Sons of God.

In this chapter, Lewis wants to discuss just how Jesus is able to impart eternal life to those who believe in Him. He begins by speculating on how things would have worked if the human race had not rebelled against God and joined the enemy. He suggests two possibilities.

- Perhaps every man would have been "in Christ," would have shared the life of the Son of God, from the moment he was born.
- Perhaps the natural life (Bios) would have been drawn up into the spiritual life (Zoe) initially and as a matter of course.

But this is speculation and we are concerned with things as they are, and that is the human race has fallen.

As a consequence of the Fall, the two kinds of life are now not only different (no problem here, this is purposeful), but actually opposed (this is the problem).

The natural life in each of us is:
- Something self-centered, something that wants to be petted and admired.
- Something that wants to take advantage of others, to exploit the whole creation.
- Something that wants to be left to itself; to keep well away from anything better or stronger or higher than it, anything that might make it feel small.
- Something afraid of the light and air of the spiritual world.

And since the natural life is in opposition to the spiritual life, it knows:

- If the spiritual life gets hold of it, all its self-centeredness and sell-will will be killed.
- Thus, it is ready to fight tooth and nail against the spiritual life to prevent this.

Lewis asks us to think back on our childhood and to imagine what it would be like if one of our toy soldiers actually came to life—a tin soldier turning into a real live man. How might the toy soldier react?
- He might not like it at all. He might think the flesh was spoiled tin.
- He might think you are killing him. He will do everything he can to prevent you.
- He will not be made into a man if he can help it.

Well, this is descriptive of our rebellion against God. And here is what God did to heal things:
- The Second Person in God, the Son, became human Himself; was born into the world as an actual man—a real man with all the natural features of men.
- The Eternal Being, who knows everything and who created the whole universe, became not only a man, but before that a baby, and before that a fetus.

And the result of this was:
- You now had one man who really was what all men were intended to be: one man in whom the created life, derived from his mother, allowed itself to be completely and perfectly turned into the begotten life.
- The natural human creature in Him was taken up fully into the divine Son. Thus in one instance humanity had, so to speak, arrived; had passed into the life of Christ.

Because the problem for us is that the natural life has to be, in a sense, killed or put to death, He choose to live His earthly life in a way which involved the killing of His human desires at every turn:
- He lived a life of poverty.

- He was misunderstood by His own family.
- He was betrayed by one of His friends.
- He was taunted, beaten, and killed by the authorities.

But then the human creature in Him, because it was united to the divine Son, came to life again! The Man in Christ rose again, not only the God.

The Difference

What, then, is the difference which He has made to the whole human race? The business of becoming a son of God, of being turned from a created thing into a begotten thing, of passing over from the temporary biological life into timeless spiritual life has been done for us. And here is what this means:
- Humanity is now saved in principle. But we must individually appropriate that salvation for it to be effective.
- We do not have to try to climb up into spiritual life by our own efforts; it has already come down into the human race.

And how do we appropriate this new life? Remember what Lewis wrote about "good infection?" One of our own race has this new life; if we get close to Him, we shall catch it from Him.

There are many ways of expressing this. We might say:
- Christ died for our sins.
- The Father has forgiven us because Jesus did for us what we ought to have done.
- We are washed in the blood of the Lamb.
- Christ has defeated death.

What we don't want to do is to start quarreling with other believers because they describe the process a little differently than we do.

Summary of Chapter 5

- In this chapter, Lewis explains how "the Son of God became a man to enable men to become Sons of God" happens.
- As a result of the Fall, our natural life is in opposition to our spiritual nature. The natural life is self-centered and self-willed. It will do anything to prevent the spiritual life from subduing it.
- The Second Person of God became a man and through His perfect obedience enabled the natural man in Him to be taken up fully into His divine nature.
- If we get close to Him, we can appropriate His timeless spiritual life as our own; we don't have to try to attain spiritual life by our own efforts.
- There are many ways of describing this transaction, including Christ died for our sins and Christ has defeated death.

Questions

1. "The Son of God became a man to enable men to become Sons of God" is one of the frequently quoted lines from *Mere Christianity*. Can you explain all that is wrapped up in this phrase?
2. Lewis suggests that our natural self is self-centered, something that wants to be praised and admired, something that wants to be left on its own. Is this a fair description of what your life was like before coming to know Jesus? Give some examples.
3. Lewis also suggests that our natural self wants to keep well away from anything better or stronger or higher than it or anything that might make it feel small. Read Luke 5:1-10. Does Simon Peter's response to this miracle of Jesus confirm what Lewis is telling us about ourselves? About you?
4. The illustration of the toy soldier becoming a real man really communicates our own rebellion against God. Can you identify with the soldier's responses? In what ways? Aren't you glad that God doesn't let us have our own way in this regard?

5. Do you see how the life of humility and obedience which Jesus lived actually killed the natural desires of His humanity? Do you agree that no man who ever lived has come anywhere close to living such a self-sacrificing life? Do you understand that God offers you this quality of life as His child?
6. What does Lewis mean that "humanity is now saved in principle?" What is the difference between being saved in principle and being saved in fact?

6. Two Notes

In this chapter, Lewis addresses two concerns which are likely to arise from the discussion in the previous chapter, namely, (1) Why didn't God just create spiritual sons in the first place, and (2) individual human beings are as important as the human race taken together.

Spiritual Sons

Someone apparently wrote Lewis after hearing his presentation of the material in Chapter 5 with the question, "Why, if God wanted sons instead of toy soldiers, did He not beget many sons at the outset instead of first making toy soldiers and then bringing them to life by such a difficult and painful process.

Lewis suggests that there is an easy answer and a difficult answer to the question.
- Here is the easy answer. The process of being turned from a creature into a son would not have been difficult or painful if the human race had not turned away from God centuries ago.
  - The reason humans were able to turn away from God in what we know as the Fall is because He gave them free will.
  - The reason He gave them free will is because a world of automata (toy soldiers) could never love and therefore never know infinite happiness.
- Here is the difficult answer. All Christians are agreed that there is, in the full and original sense, only one Son of God. If we insist on asking if there could have been many, we find ourselves in deep water.
  - For one thing, the words "could have been" do not make sense when associated with God. God is the rock bottom Fact upon which all other facts depend. It is nonsensical to ask if He could be other than what He is.
  - For another thing, the idea of God begetting many sons from all eternity is problematic. To be many, they would

have to be different from each other. But if there were several sons, they would have to be related to the Father and to one another in the same way. How then could they be different?

- Lewis confesses that his mental constructs fail him when he tries to imagine God creating several sons—he imagines them as human forms standing in space. In other words, he was mentally trying to smuggle them into the physical universe rather than them existing from all eternity.

- He then asks the sixty-four dollar question, was Nature—space and time and matter—created precisely in order to make many-ness possible? That is, was this the only way for God to get many eternal spirits—making many natural creatures in a universe and then giving them spirits.

And he admits that this is speculation and moves on to the second issue without giving an answer.

Individuals vs. Categories

The idea that the whole human race is, in a sense, one thing—one huge organism, like a tree—must not be confused with the idea that individual differences do not matter or that real people are somehow less important than collective things like classes, races, and so forth. And here is how he addresses that argument:

Things which are part of a single organism may be very different from one another; things which are not, may be very alike. Christian thought considers human individuals not as mere members of a group or items in a list, but as organs in a body—different from one another and each contributing what no other could.

- This is why we should not want to turn anyone—our children, colleagues, neighbors—into people exactly like we are. We are different organs intended for different purposes.

- And it is why we should have concern for the problems of others, remembering that though they are different from us, they are part of the same body—either the body of Christ or the human race.

And Lewis uses these distinctions to describe two errors:
- If we forget that others belong to the same organ that we do, we will become an Individualist.
- If we want to suppress differences and make all people alike, we will become a Totalitarian.

A Christian must be neither an Individualist nor a Totalitarian. And if any of us has a strong desire to tell another which of these errors is worse, it is Satan trying to divert us from the main goal. He wants us to spend our energy thinking about which is worse. Once we have decided, we will naturally gravitate toward the other.

We must simply understand that differences are important and so are individuals, and leave it at that.

Summary of Chapter 6

Lewis addresses two questions which arise from the material presented in the previous chapter:
- Why didn't God just create many sons in the first place and save us the trouble of being changed into sons by a difficult and painful process? And he gives an easy answer and a difficult answer to this question.
    - The easy answer. Had humans just followed God instead of rejecting Him in the beginning, things would have been easier on everyone.
    - The difficult answer. The process God instituted may indeed be the only way He could have created many spiritual sons.
- Differences among individuals are important and real people matter just as much as categories of people like classes, races, and so forth. If we err in recognizing this principle, we will commit one of two opposing mistakes:

- Individualists ignore the fact that all humans are part of the human race.
- Totalitarians ignore the differences from one individual to another individual.

Questions

1. The two concerns Lewis addresses in this chapter are not trivial and they would probably not occur except to someone who was really tracking with what he had to say in the previous chapter. Neither occurred to me. What about you? Did you lose any sleep over either of these issues? Can you see how they are both important?
2. Taking the first concern, Lewis gives what he calls an easy answer. Was it easy for you to understand? Was there ever any possibility, given that Adam and Eve were free agents, that they could have followed God perfectly? If not, then Lewis' answer is a non-answer. Explain.
3. His difficult answer is indeed difficult. Basically Lewis is saying that the sole reason for God creating the universe (space, time, and matter) was to provide a place for humans to inhabit as they individually undergo the process of choosing to become sons of God or declining His offer of sonship. What do you think of this proposal?
4. No one would deny that individuals are different. All one has to do to prove the point is to look at two children in the same family. Isn't it strange how we, in fact, think that everyone should be like ourselves? Why do you think this is so? It reminds one of the song from *My Fair Lady*, "Why Can't a Woman Be More Like a Man?"
5. Do you understand the difference between an Individualist and a Totalitarian? Of course we know from experience that it is difficult to maintain a balance between these two opposing positions. Do you see yourself leaning more toward one extreme? Do you understand why you need to chart an in-between course in this area?

6. Do you see how easy it would be for our enemy to cause us to favor one position over another and then be drawn toward it? Consider the labels we toss around so easily in society: conservative and liberal. Would you think that someone who identified strongly with either of these positions would fall into one of the positions Lewis has identified?

7. Let's Pretend

Pretend Sons

Lewis now wants to lay theology aside and address what we are actually to do in practice—what are to be our next steps? In order to help us understand, he reminds us of two stories, which are familiar to most people.

- *Beauty and the Beast*, which is the story of a girl who must marry a monster. When she kisses the beast, it turns into a man and they both live happily ever after.
- *The Man in the Mask*, which is a story of a man who is forced to wear a mask that makes him look nicer than he really is. Ultimately his face grows to fit it.

Lewis suggests that if we really want to see a difference in our lives we can begin by taking a shot at saying our prayers. He thinks we will begin by reciting the Lord's Prayer which begins with, "Our Father." These words, he says, mean we are putting ourselves in the place of a son of God. We are "dressing up as Christ."

- We are not like Jesus.
- What we are is a bundle of:
    - Self-centered fears,
    - Hopes, greed, jealousies,
    - Self-conceit.

Now Lewis suggests that on the human level there are two kinds of pretending:

- The bad kind, where the pretense is present instead of the real thing.
- The good kind, where the pretense leads up to the real thing.

Very often the only way to get a quality in reality is to start behaving as if you had it already.

"Dressing up like Christ" often enables us to see how the pretense could become more of a reality.

- Perhaps we become aware of thoughts that need to be controlled.
- Or we might be led to initiate some action or another.

What is happening is that Christ Himself, the Son of God, who is man (just like you) and God (just like His Father) is actually at your side and is already at that moment beginning to turn your pretense into a reality. This is not a fancy way to saying that your conscience is telling you what to do.

- Your conscience might approve of something as morally acceptable, but you know that if you wish to be like Christ, you can't do it.
- You are no longer thinking simply about right and wrong, you are trying to catch the good infection from a Person.

Jesus, the real Son of God is behind this. He is at your side beginning to turn you into the same kind of thing as Himself.

- He is beginning to inject His life, His thoughts, His Zoe into you.
- He is beginning to turn the tin soldier into a live man.

Lewis has a word for those who protest that something like this is not something they have experienced. They say:

- "I have been helped by other people."
- "But never by an invisible Christ.

If there were no help from Christ, there would be no help from other human beings. Jesus works on us in all sorts of ways, but primarily through each other:

- Sometimes through unconscious agents.
- Sometimes through unbelieving agents.
- Sometimes through the whole body of Christ, the church.

Men are "carriers" of Christ to other men—this is why showing Him to one another is so important. But we must always recognize that the Real Giver is always God—not another person.

Real Sons

Now we are beginning to see what the New Testament variously calls "being born again," or "putting on Christ," or "Christ being formed in us," or "having the mind of Christ."
- It is not reading what He said and trying to do it.
- It is Christ Himself doing things to you.
  - Interfering with your self.
  - Killing the old self.
  - Replacing it with His self.

At first it may only be for moments at a time, then for longer periods, and, finally, turning you permanently into a different sort of thing—into a little Christ which:
- Has the same kind of life (Zoe) as God.
- Shares His power, joy, knowledge, and eternity.

And soon we make two other discoveries about our life:
- We become alarmed not only about what we do, but also about what we are.
  - What one does when caught off guard is the best evidence of what sort of man he really is.
  - Resentment, vindictiveness, etc, are always present within us, but always out of reach of our conscience.
  - We can to some extent control our acts; we have no direct control over our temperament.
  - The change which we most need to undergo is a change that our own direct, voluntary efforts cannot bring about.
  - We realize that everything which needs to be done in our souls can only be done by God.
- In reality, it is God who does everything; our part is only to allow it to be done to us.

- He begins by pretending that we are not mere creatures, but His sons.
- He looks at us as if we were little Christs, Jesus stands beside us to turn us into sons.
- He treats us as if we were what we are not in order to make the pretense a reality.

But this is really not so strange. This is how the higher thing always raises the lower.

Summary of Chapter 7

When we turn from theology to practice, Lewis has some simple advice for us: to put ourselves in the place of Christ or to, as he puts it, "to dress up like Christ." When we thus pretend to be the son of God, several things happen: Jesus is at our side beginning to turn us into the same kind of thing as Himself.
- He is beginning to inject His life, His thoughts, His Zoe into us.
- He is beginning to turn the tin soldier into a live man.

At first our experience of Him may only be for moments at a time, then for longer periods, and, finally, He turns us permanently into a different sort of thing—into a little Christ which:
- Has the same kind of life (Zoe) as God.
- Shares His power, joy, knowledge, and eternity.

Questions

1. When we are adults, we inhabit the real world and leave the world of make-believe behind. Lewis thinks that pretending is important in the everyday life of a follower of Jesus. We are, he says, to pretend that we are indeed the sons of God and that in so doing, it enables Jesus to come alongside us and begin to change us from within. Do you see that pretense in this case is a good thing? Can you explain it?

2. Do you see that this is just not following our conscience? What are some things our conscience approves, but which we must not do as followers of Christ. Do you see that we really must shift from focusing on right and wrong to asking what would Jesus approve, what would advance His Kingdom?

3. Are you aware of Jesus working in your life in the way Lewis describes in this chapter? Could you share some examples? Are you aware of how God has used other believers to influence you in your walk? Unbelievers? The church? Share some examples with your group.

4. The term "Born Again" has fallen out of fashion in today's sophisticated society. Yet it is critical that we ourselves experience this reality in our lives. Suppose a casual acquaintance were to ask you if you had been Born Again. How would you respond to such a query?

5. Have you begun to pay as much attention to what you are as to what you do? Do you like what you see when you reflect on what you are? Do you agree that you are powerless to change what you are? Have you seen any evidence that God is indeed changing what you are?

6. Lewis says that God begins by treating us as if we were His sons. Is that exciting or what? Does that make you want to live as though you were a son of God? Do you see that this is no self-help project? That God does it all?

8. Is Christianity Hard or Easy?

The Christian Way

In this chapter, Lewis is going to lay out for us the difference between how the world thinks Christians live and how Christians are truly supposed to live—he called it "putting on Christ" and "dressing up" as a son of God in the previous chapter. He begins the discussion by emphasizing two important dimensions of the Christian life:

- It is not a sort of special exercise for only the very best Christians from which other Christians are excused.
- It is the whole of Christianity. Aside from the Christian life, Christianity offers nothing else at all.

Lewis continues by showing how living Christianly differs from ordinary ideas of *morality* and *being good*. The ordinary idea of Christianity which everyone has before becoming a Christian is this:

- We take as the starting point our ordinary self with its various desires and interests.
- We then admit that something else—call it *morality* or *decent behavior* or *the good of society*—has claims on this self which interfere with its desires.
- What we mean by being good is giving in to those claims.
  - Some of the things the ordinary self wants to do turn out to be what we call *wrong*—these we must give up.
  - Other things the self did not want to do turn out to be what we call *right*—and these are the things we must do.
- We are hoping all the time that when all of the demands have been met, the poor natural self will still have some chance, and some time, to get on with its own life and do what it likes.

As long as we are thinking this way, Lewis notes, one of two results is likely to follow:

- Either we give up trying to be good. If we really try to meet all the demands made on the natural self, it will not have enough

145

left over to live on. The more we try to obey our conscience, the more it demands of us. And our natural self, which is being starved and hampered and worried at every turn, will get angrier and angrier. In the end, we will either give up ...

- Or we will become very unhappy indeed. We will be one of those people who live for others but always in a discontented, grumbling way. Always wondering why the others do not notice it more and always making itself a martyr. We will be far worse off than if we had remained selfish to begin with.

The Christian way is very different—harder and easier than the worldly way.

- Jesus wants all of us. He doesn't want so much of our time and so much of our money and so much of our work. He wants everything.
- He did not come to torment and harass our natural self. He came to kill it. No half-way measures are any good.
- He wants us to hand over the whole natural self, all the desires which we think innocent as well as the ones we think wicked— the whole deal.
- He intends to give us a new self. In fact, He intends to give us His self—His self will become our self.

Jesus Himself sometimes describes the Christian way as very hard and sometimes as very easy.

- He says "take up your cross." Lewis likens this to going to be beaten in a concentration camp.
- He says "My yoke is easy and My burden light." When Jesus promises to meet all of our needs and fight all of our battles, this is easy.

So the almost impossible thing for us is to hand over our whole self—all of our wishes and precautions—to Him. But this is far easier than what we were trying to do instead:

- Remaining ourselves keeping personal happiness as our great aim in life, and at the same time trying to be *good*.

- Letting our mind and heart go their own way—centered on money, pleasure, or ambition—and hoping, in spite of this, to behave honestly, chastely, and humbly.

Living the Christian Way

Lewis warns us that the real problem of the Christian life comes where people do not usually look for it. It comes, he says, the very first moment we wake up each morning. And here is his advice for living Christianly:
- When all of your wishes and hopes for the day rush at you like wild animals, the first job each morning consists simply of shoving them all back; in listening to that other voice, taking the other point of view.
- And so on, throughout the day we are to stand back from all of our natural fussing and fretting; "coming in out of the wind" is how he puts it. We can only do this for a few moments at first, but that is how the new life spreads through our system.

Now Lewis comes back to something he wrote earlier, "This is the whole of Christianity. There is nothing else." He doesn't want us confused about the role of the Church in this. To make his case, he contrasts the role of the Church with the role of the State:
- The State exists simply to promote and protect the ordinary happiness of human beings in this life.
- The Church exists for nothing else than to draw men into Christ, to make them little Christs.

And Lewis suggests that if the Church is not fulfilling this mission, then it is a waste of time. He claims that God became Man for no other purpose than to draw men into Himself. He adds that this is also the purpose for the creation of the universe.

We have been told, he writes, how we men can be drawn into Christ—can become part of that wonderful present (redeemed mankind) that the young Prince of the universe wants to offer His

147

Father—that present which is Himself and therefore us in Him. When this happens, all will be set right.

Summary of Chapter 8

There is a great difference between how the world believes Christians live and what Lewis calls the Christian way.

- The world thinks that we start with our natural selves. Then, in the interest of morality or decent behavior, we refrain from doing anything wrong and do only what is right. Lewis rightfully shows that this approach will lead to us either giving up altogether or becoming very bitter.
- The Christian way is to give up our selves in exchange for the self of Jesus. Daily we are to submit our desires and pursuits to Him. As we learn more and more how to submit to Him, gradually His new life spreads throughout our inner being and we become more and more like Him.

Lewis thinks the great battle in the Christian life occurs during our first waking moments of each day. For it is then that we must lay aside the ambitions and desires that clamor for our attention and put on the ambitions and desires that Jesus has for us. When we begin to approach life from this perspective, Jesus is able to begin to change us from the inside out so to speak.

Lewis believes that this is the whole of Christianity—putting on Christ. And this is the responsibility of the individual Christian, the Church cannot do it for us, we must do it ourself; moment by moment, day by day.

Questions

1. Lewis has done a masterful job of describing how the world views the Christian life. We've all heard it described as having to do the ten things we really don't want to do and not being able to do the ten things we really want to do. His important contribution to our understanding is the role of the self in the

process. Do you see how we can't start with our old self? Explain.

2. Do you agree that if we try to follow the world's approach to living Christianly, we will either fail and give it up or we will become very bitter? Do you have any first-hand experience with the world's approach? Do you know of others who are following the world's approach? What could you say to them to make a difference?

3. Do you realize that Jesus wants all of you—not just some part of your time, ability, desire, or ambition? You can't hold back on Him; it is all or nothing. Can you look back on a time in your life when you gave yourself to Him lock, stock, and barrel as the old saying goes? Would you share the experience with the group?

4. Lewis rightly suggests that we can't remain ourselves keeping personal happiness as our great aim in life and at the same time trying to be good. Explain why this won't work. What does this tell us about many Americans who have as their main pursuit "personal peace and affluence" as Francis Schaeffer used to say?

5. Do you realize each morning when you awake that there is a battle raging in you between the old natural self with its desires and ambitions and the new self with the desires and ambitions of Jesus? If every morning is business as usual and you don't realize that there is a battle, what should you do about it?

6. Do you see any evidence of Jesus at work in you replacing your old self with His new self? Could you share some examples with your group? Is the age of the evidence important—that is, if the last time you saw Jesus do anything in your life was fifty years ago when you walked down the aisle of your church, is that OK?

9. Counting the Cost

Becoming Perfect

Lewis now returns to something he mentioned in the previous chapter, namely, the command to "be perfect as I am perfect." We may interpret Jesus' words here in two different ways:

- Unless we are perfect Jesus will not help us; and as we cannot be perfect, then, if this is what He meant, our position is hopeless.
- The only help Jesus will give us is help to become perfect. We may want something less: but He will give us nothing less.

Lewis uses the illustration of how when he was little and he had a toothache, he would put off going to his mother for medication because he knew that she would ultimately take him to the dentist. He knew he could not get out of her what he wanted (medication) without getting something more (the dentist) which he didn't want.

Lewis likens Jesus in our lives to the dentist. Many people come to Jesus to be cured of some particular sin:

- One of which they are ashamed—like physical cowardice.
- One which is spoiling their daily life—like anger or addiction.

Jesus will cure those; but He will not stop there. That may be all you asked; but once you call Him in, He will give you the full treatment.

This, says Lewis, is why Jesus warned people to count the cost. "Make no mistake," Jesus says, "if you let Me, I will make you perfect."

- The moment we put ourselves in His hands, that is what we are in for. Nothing less or other than that.
- We have free will, so if we choose, we can push Him away. But if we cooperate, He will see the job through.
  - Whatever suffering it costs us in this life.
  - Whatever purification it takes in the future life.

- Whatever it costs Jesus to accomplish it.

He will never rest, or let us rest, until we are literally perfect. Until His Father can say without reservation He is well-pleased with us, as He was well-pleased with Jesus. Jesus will not do anything less.

And Lewis admits that he is amazed at the patience of the Helper.
- In the long run, He will be satisfied with nothing less than perfection, but,
- He will be delighted with the first feeble, stumbling effort we make tomorrow.

God is easy to please, but hard to satisfy.

Practically Perfect

From the standpoint of practical application, this has two important implications:
- God's demand for perfection need not discourage us in the least in our present attempts to be good, or even in our present failures. He knows perfectly well that our own efforts are never going to bring us anywhere near perfection.
- We must realize from the outset that the goal toward which He is beginning is absolute perfection. And no power in the whole universe, except ourselves, can prevent Him from taking us to that goal.

If we don't understand this, then we are likely to pull back and start resisting Him after we reach a certain point. When He has enabled us to overcome a couple of sins, we might decide:
- We are now good enough. He has done all we wanted Him to do—we just wanted to become decent, ordinary folks.
- Now we would be obliged if He would leave us alone. After all, we never expected to become saints.

151

And when we say this, we think we are being humble. But this is a fatal mistake. The question is not what we intended for ourselves to become, but what He intended us to be when He made us.

- We are the creation—the machine. We may be content just to be what we call ordinary people.
- He is the inventor. He may have a very different plan for us and this is what is important.

To shrink back from His plan is not humility; it is laziness and cowardice. To submit to it is not conceit; it is obedience.

Here is another way of putting the two sides of the truth:

- We must never imagine that our own unaided efforts can be relied upon to carry us through even the next twenty-four hours as "decent" people. If He does not support us, not one of us is safe from some gross sin.
- No possible degree of holiness or heroism which has ever been recorded of the greatest saints is beyond what He is determined to produce in every one of us in the final analysis.

This is why we mustn't be surprised if we are in for a rough time. When we first turn to Christ, things seem to go pretty smoothly for a time.

- However when trouble comes along as it inevitably will—illnesses, money troubles, new temptations—we are disappointed.
- We think these things might have been necessary to get our attention and cause us to repent in the old days, but why now?

It seems to us so unnecessary; but that is because we haven't the slightest notion of the tremendous thing He means to make of us.

The command "Be perfect" is not idealistic gas. Nor is it a command to do the impossible.

- If we let Him—we can prevent Him if we choose—He will make the feeblest and filthiest of us into the image of his Son.

- He will make us into dazzling, radiant, immortal creatures, pulsating through with energy, joy, wisdom, and love unimaginable.
- He will make us into bright, stainless mirrors which reflect back to God (on a smaller scale) His own boundless power, delight, and goodness.

The process will be long and in parts painful, but this is what we are in for. Nothing less. He meant what He said.

Summary of Chapter 9

Jesus warned people to count the cost of following Him. "Make no mistake," Jesus says, "if you let Me, I will make you perfect."
- The moment we put ourselves in His hands, that is what we are in for. Nothing less or other than that.
- We have free will, so if we choose, we can push Him away. But if we cooperate, He will see the job through.

The big question is not what we intend for ourselves to become, but what He intended us to be when He made us.
- We are the creation. We may be content just to be what we call ordinary people.
- He is the inventor. He may have a very different plan for us and this is what is important.
To shrink back from His plan is not humility; it is laziness and cowardice. To submit to it is not conceit; it is obedience.

Questions

1. Have you ever thought that this business of being a Christian could go too far? That you might come to be thought of as a Jesus freak instead of being just one of the guys? Do you understand that Jesus isn't interested in your being just one of the guys?
2. Have you ever sensed that Jesus was going too far in conforming you to His image? Have you ever caught yourself

resisting Him—perhaps it was taking a stronger stand for Him at work or maybe dealing with some issues of anger? Whatever it was, you just wanted to remain as you were without changing.

3. If you answered yes to the previous question, what is it like when you shut Jesus out of your life as it relates to His changing you? Perhaps a little like Robert Boyd Munger describes it in *My Heart Christ's Home*, "When you have come to know and love Jesus Christ, one of the worst things that can happen is to sense Him withdrawing His face and fellowship. I had to give in."

4. Aren't you grateful to know that Jesus wants to give you the full treatment—He wants you to be perfect? Wouldn't you be disappointed to learn that Jesus was OK with you just being one of the guys? It should encourage us to do whatever it takes to cooperate with Him in the process. Does it?

5. Have you ever thought about the difference between your dreams and aspirations for yourself and God's desires for you? Can you see that in your wildest imaginations, you could never see the person God intends for you to be? How does this make you feel? It should make it easier to punt your ideas in favor of His. Does it?

6. Can you recall going through unusual challenges in your life—health issues, financial issues, marriage or family issues? Instead of thinking that because you are a Christian you should be beyond all of those things what should be your attitude about trials? Can you cite Scripture to back up your argument?

10. Nice People or New Men

Christians vs. Non-Christians

Those who put themselves in Christ's hands will become perfect, as He is perfect—in love, wisdom, joy, beauty, and immortality. The change will not be completed in this life, for death is part of the process. And how far the change will have gone for any particular believer in this life is uncertain.

Lewis now turns to a question that is often asked: "If Christianity is true, why are all Christians not nicer than non-Christians?" He suggests that something reasonable and something unreasonable lie behind the question.

- The reasonable part is this: If conversion to Christianity makes no improvement in a man's outward actions—if he continues to be just as snobbish or spiteful or envious or ambitious as he was before, we have cause to suspect whether his conversion was actually real.
  - Lewis thinks it is reasonable for the outside world to judge Christianity by its results. [This is very different from judging individual believers!]
  - Fine feelings, new insights, greater interest in 'religion' mean nothing unless they make our actual behavior better.
  - When Christians behave badly, or fail to behave well, they make Christianity unbelievable to the outside world.
- The unreasonable part is this: The outside world demands not only that each man's life should improve if he becomes a Christian; they also demand that they should see the whole world neatly divided into two camps—Christian and non-Christian and that every Christian should be nicer at every moment than every non-Christian. Here's why this is unreasonable:
  - "The world does not consist of 100 percent Christians and 100 percent non-Christians." [This is not a true statement! What Lewis meant to say is that Christians are at various stages of maturity—some of them act Christianly, some of

155

them don't; and non-Christians are not all evil people, many of them are very nice people.] Consequently, it is not fruitful to compare Christians in general with non-Christians in general. If we must make comparisons we need to take specific instances.

- Now suppose we want to talk about two people in our neighborhood. When we do so, we must be sure we ask the right question. If Christianity is true, then:
  - Any Christian will be nicer than the same person would be if he or she were not a Christian.
  - Any person who becomes a Christian will be a nicer person than he or she was before.

    Christian Miss Bates may have an unkinder tongue than unbelieving Dick Firkin. This, by itself, does not tell us whether Christianity works. The question is what Miss Bates' tongue would be like if she were not a Christian and what Dick's would be like if he became one. Christianity professes to put both temperaments under new management if they allow it. What we do have a right to ask is whether Christianity, if allowed to take over, improves the individual.

- Christ, if given the opportunity, is going to transform individuals. Before He is finished with her Miss Bates is going to be very nice indeed. We must be careful not to assume that Dick is all right, and Jesus only needs to pull Miss Bates up to Dick's level. Dick needs saving every bit as much as Miss Bates.

  God is waiting and watching for something in both Miss Bates and in Dick Firkin. It is something they can freely give Him or freely refuse Him. Will they, or will they not, turn to Him and thus fulfill the only purpose for which they were created?

  The question on which everything hangs is will Miss Bates and Dick offer their natures to God? The question of whether the natures they offer or withhold are, at the moment, nice or nasty ones, is of secondary importance. God can see to that part of the problem.

156

- Of course God regards a nasty nature as a bad and deplorable thing. And He regards a nice nature as a good thing. But these are good things which He gives and we receive.

  ▪ God created Dick's sound nerves and good digestion and there is plenty more where they came from.

  ▪ It costs God nothing, as far as we know, to create nice things; but to convert rebellious wills cost His crucifixion.

There is a paradox here:

  ▪ As long as Dick thinks his niceness is his own, and just as long as he thinks that, it is not his own.

  ▪ It is when he realizes that his niceness is not his own but a gift from God, and when he offers it back to God, then it begins to be his own.

The only things we can keep are the things we freely give to God. What we try to keep for ourselves is just what we are sure to lose.

Imperfect Christians

We must not be surprised if we find among the Christians some people who are still nasty. And, in fact, there is a reason why nasty people might be drawn to Christ in greater numbers than nice ones. He seemed to attract such awful people. What about the "pretty people?"

- One of the dangers of having a lot of money [we often call them the beautiful or pretty people] is that you might be quite satisfied with the kinds of happiness money can give and so fail to realize your need for God.
- Natural gifts carry the same danger. If you have sound nerves and intelligence and health and popularity and good upbringing, you are likely to be quite satisfied with your character as it is. Why drag God into it?

157

Often people who have all these natural kinds of goodness cannot be brought to recognize their need for Christ at all until, one day, the natural goodness lets them down and their self-satisfaction is shattered.

On the other hand, it is very different for the nasty people—the little, low, timid, warped, thin-blooded, lonely people or the passionate, sensual, unbalanced people.

- If they make any attempt at goodness at all, they learn, in double quick time, that they need help.
- It is Christ or nothing for them. It is taking up the cross and following—or else despair.
- They are the lost sheep. He came especially to find them. They are the "poor" and He blesses them.

There is either a warning or an encouragement here for every one of us.

- If you are a nice person—if virtue comes easily to you—beware! If you mistake for your own merits what are really God's gifts to you through nature, and if you are content with simply being nice, you are still a rebel and all those gifts will only make your fall more terrible, your corruption more complicated, your bad example more disastrous.
- But if you are a poor creature—poisoned by a wretched upbringing in some house full of vulgar jealousies and senseless quarrels—saddled, by no choice of your own, with some sexual perversion—nagged day in and day out by an inferiority complex—do not despair. He knows about it. You are one of the poor whom He blessed.

Niceness—wholesome, integrated personality—is an excellent thing. We must strive for it by all honorable means. But we must not suppose that if we succeed in making everyone nice, we should have saved their souls.

A world full of nice people, content in their own niceness, looking no further, turned away from God, would be just as desperately in need of salvation as a miserable world—and might even be more difficult to save.

Mere improvement is not redemption, though redemption always improves people even here and now and will, in the end, improve them to a degree we cannot yet imagine.

- God became man to turn creatures into sons; not simply to produce better men of the old kind but to produce a new kind of man.
- It is not like teaching a horse to jump better and better, but like turning a horse into a winged creature!

If what you want is an argument against Christianity, you can easily find some stupid, unsatisfactory Christian and say:

- "There goes your new man?"
- "Then give me the old kind."

But if you have come to believe that Christianity is probable on other grounds [logical, reasonable], you will know in your heart that this kind of straw-man argument is only evading the issue.

One soul in the whole creation you do know, and it is the only one whose fate is placed in your hands. If there is a God, you are, in a sense, alone with Him. You cannot put Him off with speculations about your next door neighbor or memories of what you have read in books.

Summary of Chapter 10

"If Christianity is true, why are all Christians not nicer than non-Christians?" Lewis suggests that something reasonable and something unreasonable lie behind the question.

- The reasonable part is this: If conversion to Christianity makes no improvement in a man's outward actions—if he continues to be just as snobbish or spiteful or envious or ambitious as he was before, we have cause to suspect whether his conversion was actually real.

159

- The unreasonable part is this: The outside world demands not only that each man's life should improve if he becomes a Christian; they also demand that they should see the whole world neatly divided into two camps—Christian and non-Christian and that every Christian should be nicer at every moment than every non-Christian. He gives three reasons why this is unreasonable.
  - It is not helpful to make comparisons between Christians and non-Christians as categories.
  - If we want to discuss individuals, only two propositions are allowed:
    - Any Christian will be nicer than the same person would be if he or she were not a Christian.
    - Any person who becomes a Christian will be a nicer person than he or she was before.
  - Christ, if given the opportunity, intends to transform individuals.

Given this background, we should not be surprised to find 'nasty' Christians—those with imperfect natures.
- Those who are blessed with money or looks or popularity are warned that it is easy to be satisfied with one's character as it is and not see the need for Christ.
- Those who suffer from character defects are often reminded of their imperfections and, thus, their need for a Savior.

Questions

1. Have you ever speculated along the lines of "If Christianity is true, why are all Christians not nicer than non-Christians?" We certainly don't have to look farther than our own selves to realize that there is abundant reason to ponder the question. Can you think of some non-Christians who put you to shame with their lives?
2. Do you understand the reasonable basis for this question? Why wouldn't we expect someone who gave his or her life over to Jesus to become a nicer person? And what do we naturally

160

want to conclude about someone who professes to be a Christian and simultaneously gives evidence of un-Christian behavior?

3. Lewis is a little sloppy here with his characterization of individuals who "are slowly ceasing to be Christians" and those who are "slowly becoming Christians." Do you understand why I maintain that his comment that the world does not consist of 100 percent Christians and 100 percent non-Christians is wrong? Explain.

4. Lewis has done a great thing by suggesting that the only two propositions we should allow in talking about the behavior of specific individuals are these: (1) Any Christian will be nicer than the same person would be if he or she were not a Christian and (2) Any person who becomes a Christian will be a nicer person than he or she was before. Do you agree? Why or why not?

5. Then what would you say to me if I volunteered that I have two neighbors, one a Christian who beats his wife and his dog, and another an atheist who is the kindest person in the neighborhood? Be sure to invoke the propositions in question 4 above in giving your answer.

6. Jesus is not in the personal improvement business; He is in the personal transformation business. As Lewis puts it, we are not talking about teaching a horse to jump farther; we are talking about a horse that can fly. Suggest some evidences of transformed character attributes you have personally experienced.

11. The New Men

The Next Step

In the last chapter, Lewis likened the work of Christ in giving spiritual life to men to that of turning a horse into a winged creature—it isn't mere improvement but Transformation. He continues by wondering what the next step in the development of man will be [He calls the process evolution, and we will go along with this analogy.] So he wants now to answer the question, "What is the Next Step? When is the thing beyond man going to appear?"

He suggests that some imaginative writers have tried to picture this next step. But they get it wrong he thinks.

- This Superman—as they call him—usually turns out as someone a good deal nastier than man as we know him.
- And they try to make up for his adversely altered disposition by adding extra legs or arms to his physical being.

Suppose the next step was something dramatically more different from the earlier steps they had dreamed of. Lewis thinks that it is very likely that it would be. He thinks the next step will be characterized by the following:

- It will be unimaginable.
- It will be different in a new way.
- It will be produced in a new way.
- It will hardly be noticed.

And Lewis suggests that the Christian view is precisely that the Next Step has already appeared. It is not a change from brainy men to brainier men; it is a change that goes off in an entirely different direction—a change from being creatures of God to being sons of God. And the first instance appeared in Palestine two thousand years ago in the person of Jesus Christ.

This New Step differs from all previous steps [in the evolution of man] not only in coming from outside nature but in several other respects as well.

- It is not carried on by sexual reproduction. As Lewis has pointed out, it comes about by association with Jesus—good infection he calls it.
- At earlier stages living organisms have either no choice or very little choice about taking the new step. But the step from being creatures to sons is voluntary.
- Jesus is more than just the first instance of the new man; He is the origin and the center and life of all the new men.
- This step is taken at a different speed from the previous ones. All of the new men have appeared in the last two thousand years.
- The stakes are higher. God has prepared man to the point where he can now transcend nature and become a son of God. Will he accept the offer?

Lewis notes in passing that the world, which thought it had stamped out this new idea with the crucifixion of Jesus, has been disappointed. It has been subsequently disappointed by the rise of anti-Christian movements—Islam, the materialism of science, and godless political schemes including fascism and communism.

Recognizing the New Men

The new men are dotted here and there all over the earth. Every now and then one meets them. What are they like?

- Their voices and faces are different: stronger, quieter, happier, and more radiant. They begin where most of us leave off.
- They are not like our ideas of 'religious' people.
  - They do not draw attention to themselves.
  - You think you are being kind to them when they are really being kind to you.
  - They love you more than other men do, but need you less.

- They seem to have a lot of time; you will wonder where they get it.

When once you have recognized one of them, you will recognize the next one much more easily. And Lewis thinks they will recognize one another immediately and infallibly, across every barrier of color, sex, class, age, and creed.

These new men are not, in the ordinary sense, all alike. One might think, based on what Lewis has written in this last book, that they would all be alike.
- To become new means losing what we now call 'ourselves.' Out of ourselves into Christ we must go.
- His will is to become our will and we are to think His thoughts—to have the mind of Christ as the Bible says.

Lewis uses two illustrations to help us understand that we are uniquely related to Jesus and to one another at once.
- Imagine a lot of people who have always lived in the dark. We might try to explain to them what light is like. If we suggested that light reflecting off of someone or something causes the thing to become visible, would that be helpful? Would they upon hearing this conclude that they would all appear identical? Possibly, but we know that the light would reveal their differences.
- Suppose a person knew nothing about salt. If you gave him a pinch to taste, he would experience a strong, sharp taste. If you then told him that salt is used to season foods, he might think that all foods so seasoned would taste the same—their taste being overpowered by the salt. But we know that the right amount of salt rather than overpowering actually enhances flavor.

It is something like these examples with us and Christ.
- The more we get what we call ourselves out of the way and let Him take us over, the more truly ourselves we become.

164

- There is so much of Him, that even residing in millions of His followers He is still not expressed to the full extent.
- Our real selves are all waiting for us in Him. It is no good trying to 'be myself' without Him.
- The more I resist Him and try to live on my own, the more I become dominated by my own heredity, upbringing, surroundings and natural desires.

What I proudly call 'Myself' becomes simply the meeting place for sequences of events which I never started and which I can never stop.
- My wishes become merely the desires caused by my physical nature or suggested to me by other men [or devils].
- What I regard as my own personal political ideas will simply be the result of propaganda to which I am exposed.

I am not, in my natural state, nearly so much of a person as I like to believe; most of what I call 'me' can be very easily explained. It is not until I turn to Christ, when I give myself up to His Personality, that I begin to have a personality of my own. Until you have given yourself up to Him, you will not have a real self.

Your real, new self will not come as long as you are looking for it. It will come when you are looking for Him. Here is the principle restated:
- Give yourself up and you will find your real self. Lose your life and you will save it.
- Submit to death, death of your ambitions and wishes every day and death of your whole body in the end.
- Submit with every fiber of your being and you will find eternal life.

Look for Jesus and you will find Him, and with Him everything else thrown in.

Summary of Chapter 11

The work of Christ in giving spiritual life to men isn't mere improvement but Transformation. "What is the Next Step? When is the thing beyond man going to appear?" The Next Step has already appeared.
- It is not a change from brainy men to brainier men.
- It is a change that goes off in an entirely different direction.
- It is a change from being creatures of God to being sons of God.

And the first instance appeared in Palestine two thousand years ago in the person of Jesus Christ.

How will we recognize that we ourselves have been transformed into new men?
- To become new means losing what we now call 'ourselves.' Out of ourselves into Christ we must go.
- His will is to become our will and we are to think His thoughts—to have the mind of Christ as the Bible says.

It is not until I turn to Christ, when I give myself up to His Personality, that I begin to have a personality of my own. Until you have given yourself up to Him, you will not have a real self.

Your real, new self will not come as long as you are looking for it. It will come when you are looking for Him.

Questions

1. Lewis calls the process of bestowing spiritual life upon man Transformation. It is not improvement. Do you agree that many people are trying to find spiritual answers by improvement? They think Christianity is a self-improvement program—if we can just make ourselves a little better, we will be acceptable to God. What is wrong with this idea?
2. The way Lewis puts it is classic. It is not a change from brainy men to brainier men; it is a change that goes off in an entirely

different direction—a change from being creatures of God to being sons of God. Do you see the difference between being a creature of God and a son of God?

3. When you hear someone say, "Well we are all children of God," you can rest assured that they probably don't get it. Everyone who has ever lived is one of God's creatures. What does it take before one can rightfully say "I am a child of God—one of His children?"

4. Lewis says that transformed people will seem to have more time than other people. This is a loaded statement. What does he mean? We all know that everyone has the same amount of time—128 hours per week. How can Christians appear to have more time than others?

5. Another astounding statement Lewis makes here is, "It is not until I turn to Christ, when I give myself up to His Personality, that I begin to have a personality of my own." Do you believe this for yourself? Have you experienced it personally? Do you think very many people today understand this truth?

6. Two times in the concluding paragraphs Lewis tells us to look for Jesus. What does he mean by this? It brings to mind what Jesus told Peter in the last chapter of John's gospel, "Follow Me." If you are interested in finding your real self, if you want to discover life, you must lose yourself in Jesus. Follow Him, that is the way to Mere Christianity.

Made in the USA
Lexington, KY
08 January 2013